Barotsela:

eight years among the Barotse

D. E. C. Stirke

Alpha Editions

This edition published in 2024

ISBN : 9789366384122

Design and Setting By
Alpha Editions
www.alphaedis.com
Email - info@alphaedis.com

Contents

PREFACE BY THE AUTHOR.

In presenting this book to the public I would like to register my appreciation of the kindness of various friends who have materially assisted me in its production. My brother-officials Messrs. Helm and Palmer and my friend the Rev. V. Ellenberger, of the Paris Huguenot Mission, have greatly assisted me with advice and information, while my sincere gratitude is due to Mr. Coxhead (Secretary for Native Affairs), Mrs. Marshall, Mr. Walton (Assistant Native Commissioner), and Mr. Thomas (Vice-Principal of the Barotse National School) for photographs.

The greatest care has been taken in checking and rechecking any and all portions of the book and several items have been deleted as lacking confirmation, which was unavoidable in handling such a mixed race as the present day Barotse.

I would also wish it to be fully understood that this work has been compiled by me, aided by my friends as mentioned before, but with no official assistance from the Administration, and this work must in no way be considered "Official" or "Approved by the British South African Co." The information to be found in the book is however fairly accurate, in spite of not being written under the ægis of the Administration.

Since finishing the book the death of the Paramount Chief Lewanika has occurred, and he has been succeeded in his position by his eldest son, Yeta, who has taken the title of Yeta II.

Lewanika was a man of about 70 years of age, and had a hold on his people that no Murotse chief will ever have again. He will, for generations, be remembered as the chief who did most for the improvement and consolidation of his people. Lewanika travelled to England for the late King Edward's coronation, and it was always a great delight to him to talk about the friends he made and the sights he saw while going to, staying in, and returning from England.

Early in his reign he was deposed by a relative of his named Tatila; but Tatila had not the grip over his people nor the statesmanship to hold the chieftainship, with the result that Lewanika was reinstated after a couple of battles. To the surprise of all he showed great clemency and pardoned most of the rebels. A notable example of his clemency is the induna Noyōō, who was very prominent in killing off Lewanika's women and children during Tatila's brief rule. Lewanika told me himself that his reason for sparing Noyōō was because he and Noyōō had herded cattle together when very small boys.

Lewanika led many successful raids against the neighbouring tribe of the Mashukulumbwe, and he was the first Barotse Chief who accepted their homage and counted them as a portion of his people.

He had a great belief in acquiring knowledge of other native races and chiefs, and sent embassies to Chitimukulu the Awemba Chief and to Khama the Bamangwato Chief (the Bamangwato being better known nowadays under the general term Bechuana).

Lewanika was a man of most charming and courteous manners and had always a very sincere regard for Europeans, while his loyalty to the Empire has repeatedly proved itself, more especially since the beginning of the German War. A visit by a European, accompanied by his wife, was always considered a great compliment by the late chief.

Missionaries always received support from Lewanika, and were given grants of land for their stations and many other privileges. The Chief himself never professed Christianity, but set an example to his people by attending church services and by supporting the Missions generally.

D. E. C. S.

INTRODUCTION.

By Sir HARRY JOHNSTON, G.C.M.G., K.C.B.

Sometime H.M. Commissioner, &c., for Northern Zambezia.

Barotseland at the present day is mainly defined as the kingdom of the recently dead Lewanika which lies both to the east and west of the Upper Zambezi, north of Sesheke, the Katima Rapids, the "Caprivi" boundary line of former German South West Africa. The western boundary line of Barotseland is the east bank of the Kwando river up stream to its intersection with the 22nd degree of E. longitude; the northern boundary is the 13th degree of S. latitude; and the eastern limit is a line drawn from the 13th degree of S. latitude to the upper waters of the Kabompo-Lulafuta, and then southward to the Majili river and along the Majili down to its union with the Upper Zambezi near Sesheke.

The master people, still, in this Upper Zambezi state are the A-luyi, who seem to have entered the lands of the Upper Zambezi from the direction of Eastern Angola, if vague tradition be anything to rely on. At any rate the A-luyi became the dominant tribe in this region some three hundred years ago, if not much earlier. Prior to their dominancy the Upper Zambezi regions had been invaded by terrible armies of cannibals, the "Bazimba" of Portuguese East African records and the "Giagas," "Jaggas" of Portuguese Congo and Angola history. The term "Jagga" seems to have been derived from the title Jaga, which they gave to their chiefs; amongst themselves this tribe or congeries of tribes which played such an amazing part in the history of Central Africa in the latter half of the 16th century was known either as the "Imbángala" of the middle course of the Kwango river or the Va-chibokwe, Va-kioko, Va-chokwe, Bajoko (according to Livingstone), or Ba-jok of South-west Congoland and the Kasai sources. This boiling over of the Va-chokwe—as they are nowadays termed in their original home—caused terrific, population-destroying raids to be made across Northern Angola into Luango and the Congo coast region, and southwards over Barotseland, Central Zambezia, Southern Nyasaland and Moçambique, and northwards up the East Coast to the surroundings of Mombasa. The Va-chokwe were known by several names in the Portuguese records, the Jagga, Ba-zimba, and Bambo (*sing.* "Mumbo.") "Ba-zimba" seems to have died out as a tribal name, but the Bambo still inhabit the region through which the Lower Shire flows, and the original Va-chokwe, Va-kioko, Va-chibokwe, or Ba-jok are prominent inhabitants in the basin of the extreme upper Kasai, and come into Barotseland or Angola on trading expeditions. They are a singularly independent, quarrelsome, warlike people, not unlikely to give trouble yet to the Belgian controllers of Congoland, to the British peace-keepers in North-West Zambezia, or to the Portuguese in Eastern Angola.

But though Upper Zambezia was traditionally overrun by the Va-chokwe three hundred and fifty years ago, the A-luyi seem soon afterwards to have absorbed the invasive quota of peoples and to have settled down as the rulers of Upper Zambezia till their land was first invaded from the south about one hundred and twenty years ago.

This invasion took place from the direction of Lake Ngami and the invaders seem to have been a section of the Ba-hurutse division of the Bechuana people. They reached the Upper Zambezi—traditionally—at the end of the 18th century, whether as friends or foes, tradition does not say; probably in small numbers and with no racial feud against the A-luyi. Their descendants may be the "Njenji" or "Zinzi" tribe who still speak a dialect of Sechuana and are settled rather high up the Zambezi. They seem however to have long retained the tribal name—Ba-hurutse—which became shortened into Ba-rotse.

These Ba-hurutse colonists of the Upper Zambezi valley apparently preserved some slender connection with the remainder of the great area of Bechuanaland, and had allowed news to reach the Fatherland of their tribe regarding the well-watered region in which they had made a new home. At any rate Sebituane, the son of an erratic woman chief in Basutoland, who in the second decade of the 19th century led her people forth on a mad excursion, gradually found his way to the north-west, and finally at the close of the eighteen-twenties had crossed the Zambezi and brought his followers—now called the Makololo—to the conquest of its upper valley.

By about 1840, he had conquered the A-luyi, whom he and his people called the "Ba-rotse" (Ba-hurutse), by the name of the earlier Bechuana colonists. Livingstone found him a fine-looking, copper-coloured man. "He was far and away the finest Kafir I ever saw," wrote W. C. Oswell at the time—1851; and many years afterwards (in 1890) he repeated the same thing to me. "Sebituane is a gentleman in life and manner" exclaimed his surprised guests in 1851, when they appreciated to the full his gracious and thoughtful hospitality.

One feels on reading the remembrances of Livingstone and Oswell how intense must have been their regret when a few days after their arrival this great chief fell ill with inflammation of the lungs and passed away. Sebituane's last days of life were taken up with recounting in a subdued voice (he was suffering from an old wound in the lungs) his wonderful adventures since he had first reached the Zambezi and found his way into Barotseland as a ruler. To the east of his moving horde of Bechuana or

Makololo, were the fierce Tebele Zulus under Umsilikazi or Mosilikatse,[1] who likewise strove to conquer for themselves a state in North Zambezia. The pressure of the Amandebele drove Sebituane to the more swampy regions of "Barotseland."

After Sebituane's death Livingstone and Oswell left his country, promising to return. His son Sekeletu—inferior to his splendid father in height, physique, and appearance—was placed on the throne and ruled Barotseland for some twelve years. Livingstone had returned to the Upper Zambezi in 1853, determined then to discover the whole secret of its course and of its main tributaries, and to follow up the trail of the Ba-joko traders and the "Mambari" or half-caste Portuguese, who were beginning to renew their trading enterprize with the Upper Zambezi, and ascertain if through Sekeletu's kingdom they could find their way "á contra costa"—to Portuguese Zambezia and Moçambique.

Livingstone traversed Barotseland (or Uluyi, as it was still more anciently called). Makololo porters and soldiers—some of whom were really A-luyi subjects of Sekeletu—accompanied him to São Paulo de Loanda, and turned back with him from Portuguese civilization to deliver him safely again at Sekeletu's capital, whence, after many adventures on the Tonga highlands and along the cataract-strewn Zambezi, he reached that river's delta and the settled towns of the Portuguese.

He returned in 1858 and, accompanied by Charles Livingstone and John Kirk, he once more entered Barotseland and sat with Sekeletu and his subordinate chiefs. But Livingstone had become by then more deeply interested in the problems, geographical and political, of Lake Nyasa and the Shiré river, the ravages of the Yao and Arab slave-traders, the courses of rivers west and north of the Nyasa watershed. Barotseland simmered on; scarcely visited by any European—unless it was some stray hunter who had found his way to the Zambezi. At last, in the year 1878, the pioneers of the great French Protestant Mission—notably Monsieur François Coillard—came into the Lake Ngami basin from Bechuanaland, and thence travelled to Upper Zambezi.

They found this former kingdom of Sebituane and Sekeletu ruled intermittently and disturbedly by a young chief of the old Aluyi dynasty—*Lewanika*. Sekeletu had died in 1864, and a period of struggle then arose in which the Aluyi and allied peoples, with possibly the remnant of the old settlement of the "Barotse" (Ba-hurutse), overcame the fighting caste of the Makololo, killed the males and married the females; and at the end of the struggle—about 1870—-the former dynasty of Aluyi chiefs was re-established.

The French Protestant missionaries (some of whom were Swiss) did much to keep Lewanika and his people in touch with British South Africa, after they were well-established in his country. He was made aware, at the close of the 'eighties, of German ambitions, of Portuguese desires to "protect" his territory—the journeys of Serpa Pinto and Capello and Ivens (1878-1883) had kept him advised of this; and at the same time of the formation of a great Chartered Company which had come to terms with the Matebele Zulus and was extending British political influence over the regions north of the Zambezi.

The "Barotse" people had heard something about the Arabs far back in the 19th century, for Livingstone found an intelligent, enquiring, civil-spoken Arab staying at or near the Barotse capital on the Zambezi in 1855.

Lewanika came to hear of the war with the Arabs in Nyasaland and on Tanganyika into which Germans and English were led, and his sympathies lay with the Europeans. Though Sekeletu had been a slave-trader on rather a considerable scale, Lewanika held such a policy in abhorrence. In 1891 he came to a preliminary understanding with the Chartered Company which has been strengthened by later agreements. In 1902, Lewanika, who had been born and brought up in the heart of Central Africa, travelled *via* Cape Town to England and was present at the coronation of King Edward VII. He looked a fine and imposing figure in Westminster Abbey, where I—recently returned from Uganda—was presented to him, after the ceremony was over. He had, indeed, as the author of this book says in his introduction, "most charming and courteous manners." Further, it should be added that in regard to the kingdom of the Barotse, the British South Africa Chartered Company has taken no false step, has incurred no unfavourable criticism, and has received praise for its control of native customs and defence of native rights from the French Protestant and the Church of England missionaries at work in this country and its neighbour states.

The Barotse country, as defined on the sketch map accompanying this book, includes a number of interesting and distinct Bantu languages. It is even possible that a traveller who pushed his explorations to the south-western limits of the kingdom and of the British sphere might find in the valley of the Kwando river a few nomad Bushmen of more normal stature than the stunted Bushmen of Cape Colony, but speaking a tongue of Bushman and not Bantu affinities. The Bushmen were more anciently inhabitants of this land than the Bantu Negroes; but not far away, to the east of Barotseland, we have had a sensational discovery within the last twelve months of a different and peculiar species of man which once inhabited South Central Africa, prior to the penetration thither of the Negro sub-species. This was *Homo rhodesiensis*, the skull, jaw, and limb-bones of which were found in close association with rudely-chipped quartz knives and scrapers, and with the broken bones of antelopes still living in Rhodesia. The place of discovery was some sixty feet below the surface in a cave at the Broken Hill Mine almost in the middle of Northern Rhodesia. The bones found are attributable to at least two personages, the limb-bones and the skull having belonged to a tall man perhaps not less than six feet in height. He possessed tremendously-developed brow ridges, a feature in which Negro man is as a rule more deficient than the European. These, and the large flat face and comparatively small front teeth and other features, suggest an affinity with Neanderthal man (*Homo primigenius*) of Europe. Other points show some resemblance to the black Australian. But the brain-case measured in space only about 1,280 cubic centimetres—a capacity much inferior to the ordinary brain-cases of the Neanderthaloids and Australoids, though, of course, there are occasional examples of Australoid women's skulls that have a brain capacity of under 1,000 cubic centimetres.

These bony remains of Rhodesian man may have been living creatures as much as forty thousand or as little as ten thousand years ago: there is not enough surrounding evidence to fix the date of them more precisely. All we can say is that the bones of the beasts they hunted and ate are nearly if not quite identical with those of existing species. Probably at the time when this big-browed, gorilla-faced man was alive, the Upper Zambezi, which flows through Barotseland three or four hundred miles westward of Broken Hill Mine, formed a great longitudinal lake in the heart of the Barotse[2] country, the greater part of which still remains very swampy. And when it issued from this expansion it joined the Kwando, the Okavango, and the Zuga to form a vast lake in what is now the North Kalahari Desert. The Guay river was then the Upper Zambezi and the Kafue river joined it as now.

The Kalahari Desert which well nigh ruins the north-western part of South Africa is probably "younger" as a desert even than the Sahara—and the Sahara Desert is a thing of yesterday, possibly much more recent than the existing human species. In the days when Rhodesian man with the huge brow-ridges, long, ape-like face and poorly developed brain ranged across all of Northern Rhodesia that was not under water, he might have passed between the vast Zambezi Lake on the west and the sources of the Guay on the east, and have wandered down into a green, tree-besprinkled South Africa, where he was no doubt killed out by the smaller but far more cunning Bushman or the intelligent Strandloopers who painted pictures on the rock surfaces like their relatives of Europe, the Crô-Magnon men. Long after these antecedent types of invaders had died away came in the vigorous Negroes...? Two thousand years ago? ... who spoke Bantu languages. Whether, between the Strandloopers, Bushmen and Hottentots who invaded the southern portion of South Africa thousands—who yet can say how many?—of years ago and the Bantu Negroes of yesterday (so to speak), other races entered and dwelt in southern and South-Central Africa, we do not know. I have given reasons elsewhere for premising that the flocking south from Equatoria of the Zulus, Bechuana, Karaña, Nyanja, Tonga, Luyi, Hérero, Angola, Luba, Lunda, Yao and Makua tribes and their allies and embranchments was quite a recent episode in the history of Africa, perhaps not more than two thousand years old. We have at present absolutely no knowledge of the incoming of any other type of inhabitant later than the Hottentot and before the Bantu; though there may have been many Negro immigrants belonging to neither group linguistically.

Barotseland, as its recent past becomes revealed to us from the second half of the sixteenth century, seems to have had as a dominant people the *Aluyi*; and as other tribes of importance the *Tonga* group (Ila-Tonga-Subia) in the south and south-east, the *Luena* or *Lubale*, *Mbunda*, and *Lujazi* tribes of northern Barotseland and the adjoining parts of Angola, the *Nkoya-Mbwela* peoples of eastern Barotseland; and a section of the southern *Luba* folk. Sporadically there has also occurred a strong invasion of the *Lunda* people (Ma-bunda) into the northernmost basin of the Zambezi, but it is doubtful whether these immigrants penetrate into the political limits of Barotseland. Similarly a section of another vigorous South Congo people has colonized the Northern Zambezi basin; the Luba, who are known in North-Eastern Barotseland as the *Kahonde* or *Kaondi*. Then again the enterprising, uppish, cheeky *Va-chokwe* or "Ba-joko" traders—once the slave-traders of South Congoland and Eastern Angola—circulate through Northern Barotseland and add yet another type of Bantu language to its markets and meetings.

The dominant language at Court and in trade to-day is an almost artificially-manufactured tongue which had come into existence during the last fifty years—*Si-kololo*. This will be found illustrated in its most modern form in the first volume of my *Comparative Study of the Bantu and Semi-Bantu Languages* (Oxford, 1919). My information has been mainly derived from the *Sikololo Grammar and Vocabulary* published in London by Dr. Stanley Colyer in 1917, and from a *Sikololo Phrase-book* produced two years' earlier by Mr. Stirke, the author of this book, in conjunction with a very noteworthy colleague, Mr. A. W. Thomas, formerly master of the Barotse National School.

Sikololo which has gradually displaced and superceded the Sechuana or Sesuto language of the original Bechwana invaders of a hundred years ago, is a far easier language to speak and pronounce than the difficult and highly peculiar idiom of Central South Africa. To philologists, Sechuana and its later southern specialization, Sesuto, are intensely interesting. Sechuana entered South Africa at as ancient a date as any other Bantu tongue—say sixteen or seventeen hundred years ago, coming thither from South-East Africa. But since then it has become highly specialized. The most specialized form of it was the southernmost, Sesuto, scarcely distinguishable a hundred or more years ago from the Sepedi of the Western Transvaal.

The chief Sebituane, born some hundred and twenty years ago, was a Mosuto, the son of a great crazy woman-chief known as Mantatisi. He carried his Sesuto tongue with him on the amazing journey he made with half his tribe across Bechuanaland to Lake Ngami and the Zambezi. Sechuana or Sesuto was the Court language in Barotseland when Livingstone first reached the Upper Zambezi in 1851. As the years rolled by, and after the Makololo (Basuto) dynasty had given place to a restoration of the Aluyi chieftainship, the original Sesuto spoken by Sebituane and well understood by Livingstone (who could converse in it freely) became greatly changed. It has remained the governing language of Barotseland and has succeeded almost in replacing and killing the remarkable Siluyi of the old rulers; and neither of the beautiful languages of the Tonga-Subia group of Southern and South-Eastern Barotseland has been allowed to take its place.

In Sikololo the pronunciation is much simplified. The rough guttural combination *kx*—of Sechuana-Sesuto gives way to the simple *k*; a hiatus formed by a dropped consonant is filled by *h*; *ts* is generally changed to *z*; *e* in the prefixes becomes *i*; *f* which had become *h* in Sesuto is generally replaced; the uncouth *tl*, *tlh* or the aspirated *th* and *kh* return to the simple *t* and *k*; and in general the pronunciation of Sikololo is brought into conformity with the harmonious phonology of the Zambezi languages.

A far more interesting tongue is *Siluyi*, the nearly extinct language of the Aluyi; in its older form, that is to say, as it was spoken round about Lialui (the original governing centre, near the left bank of the Zambezi, in about 15° 15′). Here it was a stately language, using preprefixes, and possessing all the seventeen customary prefixes of the Bantu languages. The second (*Ba-*) and eighth (*Bi-*) of these were in an abbreviated form, because the Luyi tongue had rather a dislike to an initial *b*, though it turned the sixteenth prefix—*Pa-* into *Ba-*, following a practice which recurs a good deal in the Angola tongues.

The principal form in which I have presented this language in the First Volume of my *Comparative Study* is derived from the studies of Luyi (Siluyi) compiled some twenty to twenty-five years ago by the Rev. E. Jacottet, of the French Protestant Mission. It was soon evident, when the British South Africa Co. officials got to work, that there was at least one separate dialect of Luyi spoken to the East and North-East of the main Zambezi. This was the *Si-kwango* or *Si-kwangwa*, a tongue in which the preprefixes are dropped. Si-kwangwa seems still to be a living speech among the people in the East-Central part of Barotseland; but the much nobler Luyi of the Zambezi vicinity is dying out, even among the natives of Luyi stock, dying out in favour of mongrel Sikololo.

Allied to Siluyi apparently, is the *Nyengo* language of the Bampukushu people, a scattered tribe living still (perhaps) in the South-Western portion of Barotseland, on the banks of the Kwando or Linyanti river. There has been no record of this speech since that which was compiled by Livingston about 1853, and which I have reproduced (numbered 82) in my *Comparative Study of the Bantu Languages*.

Still farther south, in the northern part of the basin of Lake Ngami, there were, down to quite recently, the *Ba-yeye* or *Makoba* people, whose language also seemed to show kinship with Luyi as well as with the Subia-Tonga group. The imperfect record of this is numbered 81 in my book. It may be extinct as a spoken tongue by now. But its existence where it last lingered on the northern side of Lake Ngami would seem to show that this basin of the shrinking lake (which received a vast but diminishing tribute of water from the Okavango river, and earlier still from the present "Upper Zambezi") was colonized by the Bantu from the north before it was found and peopled by the Bechuana tribes from the south-east.

So much does Sikwangwa differ from Siluyi nowadays, that it is almost a separate language. If this be so, the Western Zambezi group of my formation would contain at least four languages, *Yeye, Nyengo, Luyi* and *Sikwangwa*. I am also informed that Sikwangwa is not the only existing dialect of Luyi, but that two others exist, and are spoken to the North-West and North-East of Lialui and the Zambezi: *Si-koma* and *Si-kwandi*. These have only been recorded in name, and I have seen no specimens of their vocabularies. It would be interesting to ascertain whether, like Luyi, they retain the use of preprefixes; or whether they have dropped them, as have most of the languages in the western half of the Zambezi basin.

There is a tendency in Siluyi for *b* and *p* to take the place of *v* or *f* as the initial of the root, although in the prefixes *b* and *p* are inclined to drop out: so that *Aba-* becomes *Aa-*; *Ibi-*, *I*; Ubu-, Uu-; and Apa-, Aba-. Thus we have *-pumo* for "belly," instead of the familiar *-fumo*; *-bumu* for "chief," in place of *-fumu*; *-pumbu* for "ground" (ordinarily *-vu*) *-buu* for "hippopotamus" (*-vubu*), *-bula* for "rain" (*-vula*); and *-pi* for "war" (*-vita*). The roots for the numerals "six," "seven," "eight" and "nine" were in Livingstone's day, very peculiar and unlike those of any other Bantu tongue; though to-day they are supplemented by paraphrases meaning "five-and-one," "five-and-two," etc.

The Rev. Mr. Jacottet has shown how rich Siluyi was in folk-lore and legends. It is a great pity this particularly interesting, expressive Bantu tongue should be allowed to die out through the vogue given to the artificial amalgam of speech known as Sikololo.

Subia, spoken in Southern Barotseland, on and near the Zambezi at its bend eastward, is also a language of great interest, said likewise to be dying out under the rivalry of mongrel Sikololo. It was first noticed by Livingstone about 1851, and a grammatical sketch of it was given by Jacottet in 1896. But in the present century, F. V. Worthington and C. F. Molyneux, officials of the Chartered Company, supplied me with a full vocabulary and grammatical information which has been reproduced in my *Comparative Study*, Vols. I and II. Subia is spoken to the south of the Zambezi as far eastward as Pandamatenka; but it belongs to the West Central Zambezia Group, mainly in use on the north side of the great river, and including the Tonga, Ila and Lenje tongues and their dialects. This group is related to the Luba languages of Southern Congoland and to the tongues of the Bangweulu basin and of the Luangwa valley. They are all beautiful-sounding and expressive languages, representing Bantu speech in an attractive form.

The *Tonga* language is spoken in South-East Barotseland in one or more dialects. The Tonga people are a series of vigorous tribes not very likely to give up their expressive language in favour of the bastard Sikololo or the crabbed Sechuana. They attained some degree of civilization two centuries ago under the teaching of Portuguese Jesuit missionaries. Their attitude towards Livingstone and later travellers, down to the incoming of the British South Africa Company, was hostile. James Chapman, the great explorer of Southern Zambezia and even of Barotseland—in some senses the rival of Livingstone—suffered much from attacks at their hands. So did F. C. Selous. They also warred incessantly against the Zulu invasions under Umsilikazi and Lobengula, and checked the Zuluizing of central Northern Zambezia, which, in default of similar vigorous opposition, took place in the regions east of the Luangwa river.

Similarly related to Tonga and Subia are the *Ila* (Shukulumbwe) and *Lenje* tongues, though both lie almost or wholly outside the limits of Barotseland, in the central part of Northern Rhodesia. The Ba-ila tribes, two divisions of which are also known as the *Ba-lumbu* and *Ba-shala*, are a splendid-looking folk in physical development, who were long recalcitrant to European influence. In fact their healthy plateau country has only been opened up to knowledge during the last twenty years. When they were first seen in the latter part of the nineteenth century they were found to be—the men especially—living in a state of complete nudity, except in the case of the married women. But to make up for the complete neglect of clothing the men devoted particular attention to their head-hair. This was pulled up, greased, lengthened by the insertion of ancestral hair pullings, and fastened to a supple arched, recurved whip, so that it rose a foot to two feet above the occiput. Nowadays I imagine that their complete nudity is modified. The mining surveys, motor roads, and suggestions of railways, together with good and wise government, in and out of the Barotse kingdom, have succeeded in taming the Ba-ila and in drawing them into paid employment; though it is still feared by watchful administrators that they tend to diminish owing to sexual vice which causes the women to become infertile.

Another language of interest and importance is that of the *Nkoya* and *Mbwela* tribes living in East Barotseland. It has affinities jointly to the Luyi Group and to that of the North-West Zambezia languages. Preprefixes are not used, but the seventeen prefixes-with-concords seem to be fully represented in primitive forms, except that the seventh prefix (*Ki-*) is represented by *Shi-*, which brings it near to the *Si-* of Luyi. The tenth prefix is lisped as *Thi-*, *Thin-*, &c., a feature reappearing in one or two other tongues of the Group. The eighth prefix is *Bi-* and the locative prefix is *Pa-*. The root for 'two,' in the numerals is the East and South Africa form, *-bidi* or *-biji* (for *-bili*); not the *-bali* root that obtains in the other members of the North-West Zambezian Group. Another peculiarity that signalizes Nkoya is the root *-mwa-* for 'all,' only to be met with elsewhere in two of the Manyema languages of East Congoland. In Nkoya there is none of that dislike to the consonant *p*, which recurs over and over again in Bantu Africa. But in the other members of the North-West Zambezia Group this obtains, and in these—Luena, Mbunda, Lujazi and Chokwe—the 16th prefix is given as *Ha-* or *A-* instead of *Pa-*. Otherwise they are fairly orthodox, betraying little more "West African" affinities than the use of the *-bali* root for 'two' (instead of *-bili*), which is a characteristic of West Central Africa.

The *Luena* or *Lubale* language only enters the north-western part of Barotseland; *Mbunda* is spoken in separate parts on either side of the Upper Zambezi, also in the north of this state; *Lujazi* extends from South-East Angola to the western limits of Barotse territory; and Chokwe comes in as a trading language in the extreme north. None of these North-West Zambezia languages use preprefixes.

One other great Bantu Group may be met with in the northern part of Barotseland. Here there are outlying dialects of Luba and Lunda which have penetrated into Barotseland comparatively recently. The Luba tongues of South Congoland are represented by *Kahonde*, a form of South Luba illustrated in my Comparative Study under the designation of 105a. This is spoken on the North-Eastern verge of Barotseland in the basin of the Upper Kabompo river. Southern Lunda, introduced into the northern part of this territory goes under the name of "*Ma-bunda*," the root of which—*bunda*—is the same as that of "Mbunda," a quite distinct language of the North-West Zambezia Group allied to Luena, Lujazi, Nkoya, and Chokwe. "Bunda" is evidently a language and tribal name which in the shapes of -*bundu*, -*bundo*, and -*bunda* haunts Angola and Western Zambezia without implying close relationship between the different forms of speech thus termed. The "Ma-bunda" dialect of Lunda may represent an older form of the latter name, which seems to be a contraction of Lu-unda for Lu-bunda. The language (No. 111) which I have styled "Western Lunda" in my Comparative Study was originally called by its discoverer, the Revd. S. Koelle, "Ru-unda," suggesting that *Ru*- (= *Lu*-) was the familiar language prefix and -*unda* or -*bunda* the root. The loss of an initial *b* is a frequent occurrence in the Lunda languages.

The distribution of tongues southward from Angola and the Congo Basin over the regions north of the main Zambezi river indicates no causes of hesitancy, no interruptions in the north-to-south progress of the Bantu peoples. But westward of the course of the Luangwa river, as far as the Barotse country extends, or at any rate as far as the main stream of the Zambezi flows, this great river seems to have been a very decided and arresting barrier in the distribution not only of African tribes and languages but of the larger or more remarkable mammals and birds.

With regard to man of course the barrier has not been so effective. Evidently the Aluyi people of long ago crossed the Upper Zambezi and penetrate to the Lower Kwando or Chobe, and across this stream to the vicinity of Lake Ngami, though not much farther west; and in return, immigrants of Bechuana stock entered Barotseland from Lake Ngami in the last century. But there seems to have been a not easily explained halt in human migrations between Western Zambezia and South-West and South Africa. It would be comparatively easy to account for, if one could presume that the present sterile influence of the Kalahari desert prevailed two thousand or even one thousand years ago, and earlier still. But on the contrary from the many indications we can collect and from the legends of the natives in the regions south of the Zambezi, we are inclined to believe that the present arid nature of the lands on the western side of South Africa is quite a modern feature which has gone on rapidly increasing. So rapidly that even I who made a journey in 1882 to the Kunene river from Mossamedes can remember flowing streams (in the dry season) and forests, where the rivers and rivulets are now dry and the woodland is dead.

There seem, in addition, to have taken place in comparatively recent times, changes in the disposition of water supplies, which have diverted much useful moisture from inner South Africa into the Atlantic Ocean. Not such a very long time ago the Kunene river, which brings an abundant supply of fresh water from the great knot of highlands in Southern Angola, bore this water into Lake Etosha in Ovampoland, and beyond that towards the course of the Okavango or the great vanished lake of which Ngami is the surviving vestige: Ngami, which even in Livingstone's day—the end of the 'forties, some seventy-two years ago—was twice its present size. Into the same basin flowed the mighty Okavango (known much farther north as the Kubango), the Kwando and the upper Zambezi, then the outlet of another vast lake in the Barotse country. Quite possibly these two shallow lakes of huge size sent their overflow of water through the Guay river into the bed of the Zambezi-Kafue, and so out into the Indian Ocean after all; for these waters of Central Africa were completely hemmed in southwards by the plateaux of Damaraland, Bechuanaland and Matebeleland. But in those days the ultimate source of the Zambezi would have lain in the Benguela highlands near the Atlantic Ocean, and not in the Luvale country near to the upper Kasai.

As regards the mammalian fauna and some of the more striking or peculiar of African birds, Barotseland, east of the Upper Zambezi, appears, in common with all the rest of South Central Africa up to the east coast of Lake Nyasa and down to the main course of the Zambezi, to be deficient as compared with Portuguese West Africa, South Africa, and (in a lesser degree) Moçambique. It probably has more in common as a distributional area with the southern part of the Congo basin outside the forest area, and west of the Luapula-Lualaba streams. Down to recent times Barotseland possessed great herds, enormous numbers of a few species of game animals, but not such a great variety of species. Like South Congoland outside the forest zone, it seems never to have had any example of the rhinoceros: indeed, I have no confirmatory evidence of the existence of a rhinoceros or a giraffe, west of the eastern rise of the Nyasa-Tanganyika plateau, or of the waters of Lake Nyasa. The rhinoceros begins to show itself south of Lake Nyasa and east of the Shire river. It recurs in Southern Angola and Damaraland, up to the vicinity of the Western Zambezi, and as far north as the beginning of the lofty plateaux where the Kwanza river rises.

The Kwanza, which divides Angola into two unequal portions, is very noteworthy as a boundary. Its ultimate sources are in the Ngangela, Bihé and Lujazi highlands (plateaus and mountains) which connect the mountain ranges of Benguela on the west with the 5,000-feet-high plateau dividing the Southern Congo basin from that of the Zambezi. This undulating line of heights (rising on several peaks to nearly 8,000 feet) really marks off Southern from Northern Angola; and zoologically Southern Angola extends eastwards almost to the banks of the Upper Zambezi and covers the western limits of Barotseland.

Here you have a remarkable extension of the South African area of zoological distribution. East of this, from the Upper Zambezi to the Shire river and the east coast of Lake Nyasa (with the Zambezi as a southern boundary) there is an interruption in distributional area which affects certain mammals and birds very curiously. For some the interruption is complete. The Ostrich, the true Gazelles, the Oryxes, the Secretary bird, certain types of Vulture, the Striped Hyena, the Chita or Hunting Leopard, the Caracal Lynx, the Aard Wolf (*Proteles*), the Big-eared Fox (*Otocyon*), the small Desert Foxes, the Black-backed Jackal, the *Pedetes* or Cape Jumping Hare, the Elephant-shrews, the Mountain Zebras, the White Rhinoceros and, in a lesser degree, the Black, are in a measure confined to north-east and eastern Equatorial Africa on the one hand, and to Africa south of the Zambezi and to Southern Angola on the other. Some of the examples cited stretch across to the Bahr-al-ghazal and even Northern Nigeria from Abyssinia and the Eastern Sudan; others reach Senegal and Western Nigeria beyond the forest zone. But all of the examples cited (besides many more less well-known birds and mammals) seem to be absent from North Angola, Northern Zambezia and Nyasaland, and apparently also from Moçambique. In Moçambique, numerous forms may have been exterminated by the white man and the black hunters, who began shooting here in the 17th century. Yet it is difficult to understand that they could thus have eliminated the Ostrich, Springbok, Striped Hyena (represented in South Africa and Angola by the Brown Hyena), Chita, Caracal, Aard Wolf, and *Pedetes* rodent, or even the Giraffe.

The Giraffe's distribution conforms somewhat, but not so closely, to similar restrictions. Its least specialized form, perhaps, is the Reticulated Giraffe of Somaliland, whereon the original markings are seen to be white stripes, horizontal and perpendicular, on a red ground. From Somaliland the Giraffe radiates over the eastern Sudan to Northern Nigeria and thence (with gaps) to Senegal. It entirely avoids forested Central and West Africa, though it has a near relation, the Okapi, in the forests of Equatorial Africa east and north of the main Congo river. The distribution of the Giraffe continues south from Uganda and Somaliland to the east of Tanganyika and Nyasa down to the neighbourhood of the Ruvuma river. It has never been reported south of that stream, or until the Lower Zambezi has been *crossed*. A hundred years ago and down to about 1900 it was found in various sub-species and varieties *south* and *west* of the Zambezi to Cape Colony and into Southern Angola. But it has never been shown to exist between the Upper Zambezi and the Moçambique coast, north of that river system.

On the other hand the range of the Sable Antelope does not leave out Northern Zambezia and Barotseland. It begins in Eastern Africa, in the latitude and neighbourhood of Mombasa (a fact first suggested in my book on Kilimanjaro, published in 1885), broadens over what was formerly "German East Africa," passes round the south end of Tanganyika into Southern Congoland and crosses Barotseland into Eastern Angola. Here, in the south-eastern basin of the Kwanza, and possibly in north-western Barotseland as well, it develops its most superb form—*Hippotragus variani*, generally called the Giant Sable—with magnificently developed horns, longer than those of any other type found elsewhere, and a longer, narrower skull. It is possible (from heads I once saw, shot to the west of the main Upper Zambezi and specimens of horns) that the Giant Sable may be found just within the limits of Barotseland.[3]

North of the belt of dense forest between the Liba and Kabompo, on the spongy plains near to the river, Livingstone noticed in the rainy season large numbers of Buffaloes, Elands, Kudus, Roan Antelopes, Gnus, and other game. He even avers that farther north he saw a White Rhinoceros. It was on a Sunday and his encampment was almost surrounded by herds of astonished Mpala antelopes, tsesebes ("bastard hartebeests"), zebras and buffaloes. But although the Black Rhinoceros is undoubtedly found in Southern Angola close up to the Barotse frontier, and the White has been shot immediately south of the Upper Zambezi, no word has come from any other quarter as to the existence of the monstrous White square-lipped species in the direction of the Upper Zambezi and the Congo watershed; so it is possible his eye-sight was deceived.

Giant Sable Antelope, from Angola

(From a specimen in the Museum of the New York Zoological Society presented by JOHN JAY PAUL.)

In general, Barotseland, east of the main Zambezi and of its great north-western affluent the Lungo-e-bungo, seems to possess the mammal and bird fauna of Northern Angola, Southern Congoland, Northern Rhodesia and Nyasaland. Moçambique is richer—up to the Shire river—in possessing the Black (I used to think also the White, and perhaps was not wrong) Rhinoceros, and a few other creatures found also in Eastern Equatorial and in Trans-zambezian Africa. Otherwise Moçambique remains rather an unsolved problem, as to why and how it served as an interruption in the spread of the vertebrate fauna of Pliocene and Pleistocene North Africa down to South Africa, an extension which as regards West-Central and Western Africa may have been barred by the former enormous area of dense forest growth.

In botany, as in vertebrate zoology, Barotseland is part of the region which lies between the Kwanza and Zambezi rivers on the south, and the main-stream of the Congo on the north, from Lake Mweru to the Atlantic

Ocean. It has a sufficient rainfall, from 22 inches in the south-west to 42 inches in the north-east, to maintain a fairly luxuriant flora as well as powerful rivers. North of the confluence of the Kabompo and the Liambai or Liba (the Upper Zambezi), there seems to have been seventy years ago a luxuriant belt of forest stretching northwards and occupying the mountainous region between the Liba-Zambezi and the Kabompo or Lulafuta.

The average elevation of the Barotse Valley, south of this confluence, ranges from a little under 3,000 feet at Sesheke to about 3,600 feet at the juncture of the Zambezi and the Kabompo; but the forested country between these rivers must rise in part to at least 4,500 feet. The richness of this forest seems to have made an immense impression on Livingstone in the middle of the 'fifties. Up till then, coming from South Africa through Bechuanaland, he had at most seen scattered trees with occasionally a fine solitary umbrageous specimen, or a palm thicket. But above the confluence of these two rivers he evidently plunged (when he had to land) into a woodland comparable with the splendid forests of the Congo or the Cameroons. His *Missionary Travels* contains some very good word-painting of the grand growth of the trees, the deep gloom of the forest depths as contrasted with the shadeless glare of Bechuanaland. In spite of the incessantly rainy weather—and in this little-explored region the yearly rainfall must be far in excess of the modest estimate quoted by travellers in the Barotse park-land and plateaux—Livingstone found considerable pleasure in here seeing—for the first time—the *real* forest display of Central Africa.

North of the Zambezi-Kabompo junction Livingstone noticed the increasing growth of the bamboo on the uplands, as a skirting of the great display of tropical forest which so deeply impressed him as he followed the northward course of the main Zambezi. This—or these—bamboos recur on the elevated plateaux of Eastern Barotseland, and extend over a good deal of the upland on either side of the Upper Kafue, as well as over the five thousand feet crest of the Congo boundary. No doubt they may also be observed within the north-western limits of Barotseland. They are seemingly of the same types as the bamboos of Nyasaland and the elevated portions of Northern Rhodesia south of Tanganyika, and in such case belong to the *Oxytenanthera* and *Arundinaria* genera. The only other genus of *arboreal* bamboo in Africa is *Oreobambos*; but that, I think, is confined in its range to Abyssinia and the Snow mountains of East Equatorial Africa.

The forests of Northern Barotseland have one or more species of wild plantain (*Musa*) and either wild or introduced examples of the oil palm, where the rainfall is over fifty inches per annum. This may have been introduced from Congoland or Northern Angola by the natives, who in the north of the Barotse country are so closely connected with the peoples of the Congo basin; or as in the case of North Nyasaland and Zanzibar Id., it may be a separate species or sub-species of the *Elaïs* genus.

According to the reports of later travellers, there is much woodland and scrub on the higher land—4,000 to 4,500 feet—on the west side of the Zambezi, south of the Kabompo-Zambezi junction. This woodland is also repeated, less markedly, to the east of the great river where the land likewise rises. The Mankoya country (Eastern Barotseland) has a larger, steadier rainfall than Sesheke and the southern regions; and the Mashukulumbwe table-land, and the valley of the upper Kafue are said to be well and regularly watered countries. The more scattered growth of trees (occasional fine and large trees are common) seems due to human intervention. The natives of the Lukona province, towards Angola, are a wilder, less intelligent race than folk of Tonga kinship on the east, and not so eager to promote tree planting. Bulovale (the region between the Luena and Kabompo rivers) and north of the Kabompo up to the boundary of the Zambezi watershed are well forested regions.

The central valley of the Zambezi—"Borotse proper,"[4] as it might be called, the region which the Barotse (really the Aluyi) have so long dominated—ranges from below the Zambezi-Kabompo confluence on the north to the Gonye Falls on the south, and is about 150 miles long and 60 miles broad. It is the bed—most observers think—of the old lake of the Upper Zambezi, and presents to-day an utterly flat and treeless aspect. Then ensue from Gonye to Katima, some eighty miles of rapids or falls. From Katongo to Mambova, past the now world-famed Sesheke, where Livingstone and Oswell first "discovered" the Zambezi, there are fifty miles of navigable river; then two more rapids at Mambova and Nkalata, and then another navigable stretch of some sixty miles to the vicinity of the Victoria Falls. (These lie well outside the political limits of Barotseland, the boundary striking north along the Majili river, ten miles east of Sesheke.) The plain of the extinct lake is much flooded during the winter rains, when a good deal of central Barotseland is under water. The rainy season seems, however, to be tending more and more towards the spring months (the autumn of South Central Africa).

The geology of Barotseland may be summarized thus: In the north-west, north, east and south-east the surface is a red laterite clay, superimposed on granite which in the higher portions obtrudes itself in mountains and hills. The central valley and most of the south-west has a heavy, white, sandy soil, but with a good deal of alluvium laid down on the sand by river courses or in the bed of the ancient lake. There is a basaltic outbreak in the neighbourhood of the Victoria Falls, but this lies outside Barotseland limits. In the eastern half of the country gold, copper—connected with the copper deposits of Katanga—tin, lead, zinc and iron have been discovered, chiefly in regions between four and five thousand feet in altitude.

In this little book and in the first and second volumes of my *Comparative Studies of the Bantu Languages* (fed from much the same source) our information concerning Barotseland and its peoples has been greatly implemented. But that fact does not conceal from us that the country, its zoology, botany, peoples, and even its geography (to say nothing of geology) are still far too little known. The portions that lie to the west and south-west of the main Zambezi remain almost *un*known and undescribed, or are only made known to us in works of travel fifty, sixty, seventy years old, which even if accurate in what particulars they give were written at a much lower level of knowledge than exists concerning Africa in general to-day. We know more about Eastern Angola than we do of Western Barotseland. Recent discoveries concerning Angolan Antelopes, Zebras, Rhinoceroses, and other mammalian types make us eager to ascertain how these discoveries affect Barotseland *west* of the Zambezi. How far do the Bushman tribes extend into Western Barotseland? Are they of normal human stature, like those of South-East Angola? Do they speak languages akin to the Bushman tongues and use clicks? Have they greatly projecting brows like certain Bushmen of the Northern Kalahari, or are they without brow projections at all but very prognathous in the lower part of the face? What is the full tale of the Bantu tribes of Western Barotseland? Are there still unrecorded Bantu languages on the Kwando river? Do the tongues recorded south-west of the Upper Zambezi by Livingstone, seventy-two years ago, still exist?

Does Livingstone's great forest between the course of the Upper Zambezi and that of the Kabompo still maintain itself, in spite of the reckless spirit of destruction inherent in all uneducated Negro tribes, who since the imposition of peace by the white man have been largely increasing the area of their settlement in Northern Barotseland? If the forest is still there, in whole or in part, why are no botanical reports and collections available? The botany of Barotseland, in common with its zoology, has never been efficiently explored and reported on since the land was first entered. Cattle apparently prosper in the whole country; yet the tsetse fly exists seemingly everywhere. Does it, north of the Zambezi and west of the Luañgwa, convey no germs? The time—it seems to me—has come when the British Empire, from London or from Cape Town, should have this country examined scientifically from west to east and north to south; not with anything but benevolent intentions towards its natives—Aluyi and Batonga, Basubia and Mabunda, Batonga and Baila, Bankoya and Kahonde, Valujazi and Valubale—but with the earnest endeavour to make fully known its resources and defects, its wonders and survivals, and the relation that Western Barotseland bears to the growing menace of South Africa: the spread of the Kalahari Desert, the drying up of once fully habitable land, the cause of ruin in South Angola, in Eastern Damaraland, and the vast, dead region north, east, south, and west of Lake Ngami.

H. H. JOHNSTON.

The Mokwai Mataŭka of Nalolo with her husband (standing) and interpreter (sitting)

Photo by Mrs. Marshall

CHAPTER I.
The Barotse and their Origin.

The origin of the Barotse is a matter of conflicting conjecture. It has been suggested by the Abarozwi of Southern Rhodesia that the Barotse are descendants of theirs and that Lewanika is a direct descendant from their royal house. The Barotse of Barotseland deny this *in toto*. They aver that they came south from the Congo Basin and found the Alunda and Balubale living in their country (*vide* map). The Alunda and Balubale confirm the statement of the Barotse, and it is known that the Barotse lived for some years among the Lunda, gradually working south till they left the forest country on the Zambezi and came out on to the flat swampy country known to-day as the Barotse Valley.

They were then sometimes called by foreigners the Barozi or Barotse, but were better styled the A-luyi and spoke Siluyi and in our days Sirozi or Sikololo.

During the chieftainship of Mbukwano, the A-luyi were conquered by Sebituane, a roving Mosutu with a band of warriors. Sebituane not only re-christened the A-luyi as "Makololo," but forced Sesuto as a language on them. Sebituane and his followers were not called Basuto by the A-luyi but Makololo, which name, according to the Rev. E. Smith, once of the Batonga-Baila mission, was derived from the fact that Sebituane's favourite wife was a Makololo woman.

Sikololo (a mongrel form of Sesuto) is the lingua franca of the Barozi to-day. The greatest difficulty is found in getting any well-authenticated information from the Barozi as to their past history.

The origin of the name "Murozi" (a native of the Barozi country) is peculiar. The true name of the people is the A-luyi; the prefix *A* or *Ba* being the plural of *Mu* and applied to mean "people." When the Makololo under Sebituane first invaded the southern portions of the country, they found a subordinate tribe called the Masubia living near Sesheke. These people told the Makololo that their overlords living to the north were the "A-luyi." The Makololo converted this into "Ba-luizi," "Ba-ruizi" (L and R being interchangeable) and finally "Ba-rozi." Why the foreign missionaries decided to call it "Barotse" is best known to themselves; certainly no one else can imagine or find any reason for it at all. There is no possible reason for mistaking the "z" in Barozi for "ts".[5]

Whether from the vicissitudes of their southern trek or from natural laziness is unknown, but they have no system of record, nor, as is the case in many native tribes, have the village elders ever acted as historians and handed their knowledge on from father to son. The Barozi themselves say that owing to their numerous raids and their intermarriage with the aboriginal tribes and with women raided from other tribes, they have lost all purity of race and incidentally all remembrance of their former history. They certainly are to-day a very mixed race, and nearly all their songs, dances, customs and legends are either borrowed wholly or in part from other tribes. They are quite positive that the Abarozwi of Southern Rhodesia are related to them, but they state that these people are a branch that left them and trekked south into Matebeleland where they settled. If this is correct it must have been previous to the Matebele settling in Southern Rhodesia under Mosilikatse, as the Barozi, though fond of raiding weaker or more divided people, were too canny to try conclusions with a powerful and warlike people like the Matebele. Besides the raid of Sebituane and his Makololo, several raids by the Matebele are known of, and although the Barozi certainly suffered at the raiders' hands, they generally got rid of them by strategy and cunning. Their own successes over people like the Bashukulumbwe and Batonga were nearly always gained by treachery, superior numbers, superior weapons, or else by internal dissensions amongst the people they raided.

The Barozi were very fortunate in the class of people they found occupying the country they settled in; the more timid tribes were at once enslaved, while more powerful people were propitiated and gradually absorbed. Unfortunately, the conquerors readily acquired all the vicious and degraded habits of the conquered, and are to-day, both physically and morally, a far poorer type of native than they were on entering the country, always providing their statements are true. Natural laziness and the rapidity with which they acquired the demoralizing customs of their subject people have practically eliminated the true Muluyi nature in so much that the real Sirozi or Siluyi language is gradually dying out and to-day is known to but a few of the blood royal, sons of Indunas and the like. Sikololo, which is a mongrel Sesuto, is the commonest language in use in the country and even amongst the outlying tribes such as the Alunda, Balubale, Bankoya, Batotela, Bandundulu and others, it is always possible to find one or more persons in every village with a slight knowledge of Sikololo. The missionaries possibly made a mistake in not working up Sikololo on their arrival in the country, but having Sesuto text-books and grammars to hand they commenced to teach Sesuto. Sikololo is now being reverted to and this should simplify matters to a great extent. Many pure Siluyi words are in use in Sikololo, for which there are no equivalents in Sesuto. For example, river work such as paddling and other matters connected with boats are unrepresented in Sesuto, as there is no river work in Basutoland, and the words in use in Sikololo are practically all Siluyi.

One of Lewanika's Aunts with Attendant

Photo by J. C. Coxhead, Esq.

Lewanika's Band (Mirupa and Silimba)

Photo by J. C. Coxhead, Esq.

Siluyi itself is doubtless a corruption of an older Siluyi language, but this is hard to prove owing to the lapse of time and lack of authentic records.

The Bambowe, an aboriginal tribe on the Zambezi, living south of the Balunda, corroborate the statement made by Alunda and Balubale, that the Barozi or Aluyi lived amongst them while coming from the Congo Basin. The Bakwangwa, another aboriginal tribe living east of the Zambezi, say the Barozi found them there and absorbed them, and yet Sirozi (Siluyi) is clearly the language of which Simbowe and Sikwangwa are dialects. Any one conversant with one of these languages, understands and is understood by speakers of the others. Some idea of the composition of the Barozi people of to-day can be gained when one realizes that they are composed of Bambowe, Bakwangwa, Bahoombi, Bakoma, Makololo, Bandundulu, Bambunda, Bankoya, Bashasha, Alunda, Balubale, Bambalangwe, Batonga, Basubia, Mashukulumbwe, Bakwande, Batotela, Bakwangali, Bakwengo, Balojazi, Vachibokwe, Basanjo and other tribes. Many of the above tribes were, so far as can be gathered, aboriginal owners of the Barozi country, others were raided from time to time and slaves (chiefly women) taken back to the homes of the raiders, where they in time intermarried and became Barozi.

CHAPTER II.
The Administration of Barotseland.

The Barotse Reserve is administered by the British South Africa Company in agreement with the Paramount Chief Lewanika. By this agreement the Chief Lewanika has handed over certain powers and privileges to the B.S.A. Co. The company is empowered to collect a poll-tax, of which a percentage is set aside for the Barotse nation. Out of this percentage the Barotse National School and its industrial branch is maintained. The school is controlled by a European principal and vice-principal, as well as a European instructor, at the head of the industrial side, supported by an effective staff of native teachers. The B.S.A. Co. further have a resident magistrate near Lewanika's capital at Lialui, who is supported by two Northern Rhodesia police officers and a company of native police (recruited in Angoni and Awembaland). Native commissioners are maintained at Lialui, Nalolo, Balovale, Mankoya, and Lukona, with an assistant magistrate and a native commissioner at Sesheke.

Lewanika has ceded all judicial rights to the B.S.A. Co. with the exception of very minor items and of civil cases between natives. At the same time the B.S.A. Co. recognizes native laws where such native laws are not repugnant to British ideas of justice.

At present Lewanika has his capital at Lialui, where his Kotla (Parliament)[6] sits daily. His sister Mataŭka is Mokwai of Nalolo (Mokwai being a title designating a woman of royal blood on the father's side).

A younger sister, Mbwanjikana, is Mokwai of Libonda, and Lewanika's eldest son Litia (or Yeta, as he is now called by all Barozi since his youth) is stationed at Sesheke. (Yeta, styled Yeta II, has since succeeded his father as Paramount Chief.) The two sisters and Yeta are subordinate to Lewanika, but all three have their Kotlas (Parliaments) and Prime Ministers. There is a right of appeal from any of these subordinate Kotlas to the Lialui Kotla.

The Barozi Reserve is closed against farming or mining, and is reserved for the Barozi only. Trading is allowed, but any applicant for a licence has to be proved by the Administrator, Resident Magistrate, and the Chief Lewanika—Lewanika getting a half share of all gun and store licences issued throughout Barotseland.

Liquor is naturally not allowed to be sold in the Reserve, nor are powder, caps, nor guns. The Administrator will grant permission to the Chief, at his request, for any of the more important Indunas to buy sporting guns and a limited amount of ammunition.

Slavery has been suppressed, although, in due justice to the Barozi, it does not appear to have existed in its more brutal form in this country. The B.S.A. Co. has given every encouragement to the Paris Huguenot Mission in the Reserve, and the Mission have several privileges to assist them, such as free inspection of their schools by the Principal of the Barozi National School, the reservation of vacancies in the Barozi National School for members of the Mission Schools and other items. The Chief Lewanika has always lent the mission the support of his approval, although he himself has not become converted.

The B.S.A. Co. has endeavoured in every possible way to protect the interests of the Barozi people and their Chief Lewanika. The Resident Magistrate at Mongu, besides his magisterial duties, acts as adviser to the Chief and the Kotlas (or Parliament) as well. The native is safeguarded against himself as regards his cattle by restrictions placed on the local traders as to numbers purchased annually—restrictions on breeding stock being much more stringent than on bulls and bullocks. The Rhodesian Native Labour Bureau is given free access to the country to recruit labour, but is under close Government supervision.

A Lujazi Village

Photo by J. C. Coxhead, Esq.

Lewanika's Head Paddlers

Photo by J. C. Coxhead, Esq.

Besides all these safeguards, there is a Resident Commissioner stationed at Salisbury in Southern Rhodesia, a large part of whose duties is the protection of natives' rights. Beyond him again is the High Commissioner for all native protectorates, who directly represents His Majesty King George V, and is also Governor-General for the Union of South Africa.

A poll tax of 10s. is collected, which is very much lighter than the tax collected from any native race south of the Zambezi. This tax is collected from adult males only, boys, old men and women not being taxed, with the exception of second and other wives of polygamous marriages. A man's first wife does not have to be paid for, but, as a man who marries more than one wife is nearly always a man of means, he is responsible for the tax of his second and other wives. Exemptions are granted from payment of tax, either for a number of years or for life, for sickness, disease or old age.

The Administrator of Northern Rhodesia pays a visit to the Barozi Reserve in person or by proxy every year, and during his visit the Chief and the people are at liberty to bring any complaints and grievances before him. No matter is too trifling or insignificant to receive the fullest and most careful attention and it is doubtless the care taken over these minor points that has solidified the excellent relations at present existing between the Chief Lewanika and the officials of the B.S.A. Company.

CHAPTER III.
Native Administration.

The Paramount Chief of the Barozi is the head of the nation and, in the eyes of his subjects, can do no wrong. His actions are nevertheless curtailed by the national assembly, which was called in the early days of the Aluyi, the "Namōō," but after the Makololo invasion, the "Kotla."

On state occasions the Chief sits in the middle of the Kotla which holds its daily meetings in a long rectangular building open on three sides. Half-way along the fourth side, which is walled, sits the Paramount Chief on a raised daïs. On his immediate right sits the "Ngambela" or Prime Minister and the various Indunas in order of the responsibility of their positions. On the immediate left of the Chief sits Ingangwana the Induna at the head of the "Likombwa," a division of the people who supervise the Chief's food and all his personal property (as different from his property as Chief). On the left of the Likombwa sit all sons-in-law of the Chief, with the exception of those who hold positions as Indunas of the people, in which case they sit to the right in order of seniority of position.

In any discussion the "Left" supports the Chief while the Ngambela and the "Right" oppose the Chief, should his wishes clash with the national welfare. There are two rules for the conduct of business in the Kotla which will be dealt with separately. No state affairs are discussed in the presence of the Chief by the assembled Kotla. The reason for this is that out of respect for the Chief's person, it is argued that discussion would be cramped and restrained and that the best and wisest solution of the question would not be arrived at. So the arrangement of the Kotla may be placed under the following two headings: (1) with the Chief present; (2) in the absence of the Chief. (1) The Chief comes practically daily and sits in the Kotla to show himself to his loyal subjects, and to let them see that he is well. Trivial matters only are discussed, the Chief asking any questions he wishes of the Ngambela or any of the indunas.

Should there be embassies from other people, they are received while the Chief is present and the Chief may, at will, call up the head of the embassy and inquire of him as to the health of the Chief who sends the embassy, the state of crops and general welfare of the nation represented, or as to how the embassy like the Barotse country; but all these questions are polite nothings.

While the Chief is present, the Left sits as previously stated but the Right is slightly different. First comes the Prime Minister (or Ngambela), after him comes Solami. Solami is the man who represents the father of the Chief. As is easily understood no Chief, whose father held the chieftainship, ever held sway during his father's lifetime. This is not stipulated by law but has always been the case—the death of a Chief's father often having been arranged by his son to secure succession. So we find Solami is the man who has married the Chief's mother. Here again it might be suggested that a Chief's mother might also be dead by design or by course of nature. This is guarded against by the Barotse custom "ku yola" (to appoint), which appoints a successor to take the name and position of any male or female person of importance. Makoshi, the mother of the present Chief, Lewanika, died about ten years ago and a daughter of Lewanika's (Ngula by name) was at once appointed Makoshi. Her husband is Solami and, though a son-in-law, yet represents the father of the Chief.

On Solami's right sits Natamoyo. "Natamoyo" means the "father of life" according to the Siluyi meaning of the word "moyo," and he has or rather had, a position of great value and power. Should any man—Chief, induna, or private person—be pursuing anyone with the desire or intention of killing him, the hunted person was safe directly he could reach the Natamoyo or his palisade. Natamoyo was in fact very similar to the "city of refuge" of the Old Testament. Natamoyo also had the power to veto an execution when discussed in the Kotla, but his chief value lay in his being a haven of refuge. He had as well the following privilege. If the Chief committed any act of injustice to any of his people, the injured party could complain to the Natamoyo, who then went to the Chief's palisade and abused him roundly. The Chief would then desist from the course of action which was objected to. Needless to say this privilege was very great and valuable amongst a people over whom order was only maintained by the exercise of great brutality, persecution and very often injustice. It is hardly needful to point out that anyone else having the temerity to resent any action of the Chiefs would have paid for it with his life, in all probability being assisted out of the world, with torture and various most revolting cruelties.

After Solami comes Mukulwakashiku, an Induna who acts as Prime Minister during the absence of the Ngambela. On Mukulwakashiku's right sit the various indunas who take precedence by the relative value of their positions.

(2) When the Chief leaves the Kotla, the business of the people is discussed; cases are tried and new laws talked over, or old laws amended. The "Right" sits in the same order, but the positions of Solami and Natamoyo are now of little value and the two leading men are the

Ngambela and Mukulwakashiku. Other divisions of the people for legislative purposes will be described later, but the method of the procedure of the Kotla will now be given. The Ngambela calls Mukulwakashiku and instructs him to inform the assembled Kotla of the matter under discussion. This is done and the assembled Barozi are called on to express their opinions. The smallest man (in position) on the "Right" starts the ball rolling, and utters his views on the matter. He must be a free-born Murozi, but not of necessity even the headman of a village. All the divisions have different values for each member and the junior member of each division speaks first. In a large assembly the first speakers are always members of the "Ikatengo," a division which comprises the people, petty headmen and very minor indunas. Headmen of more important villages and sub-Indunas of the "Lukaya" division speak after the Ikatengo have finished. When the "Lukaya" have finished, the indunas of importance who comprise the Saa division speak next. Following them, the Sikalu expresses its opinion; this division is composed of the higher indunas. Members of the three division, Lukaya, Saa and Sikalu of the "Right" alternate with members of the "Left," and when the head "Sikombwa" of the "Left" has finished, Mukulwakashiku gives his personal opinion. He is the last speaker before the Ngambela. The Ngambela then gives a brief résumé of the various pros and cons and shows the weak points in the different arguments.

Should he disagree with the majority, a lively discussion takes place, and should the majority still disagree, the matter is laid before the Chief by one of the "Sikombwa" (Left) and his decision is final. This is seldom if ever the case—especially nowadays—as the present Ngambela is a man of great cleverness, tact and diplomacy, and can always command a great following. When the matter is settled in the Kotla, one of the "Sikombwa" is sent with word to the Chief who sends word back by the same man as to his approval or otherwise. In the event of his disapproval he gives his reasons by the same channel, and these reasons are announced to the Kotla by Mukulwakashiku at the Ngambela's orders. When the Kotla hear the Chief's reasons, they signify their agreement thereto by clapping their hands (kandelela), and their resolutions are rescinded or else they refuse to be guided by the Chief. The Ngambela then goes to the Chief and explains the matter and urges his acceptance of the ruling of the Kotla. This he generally gets.

This is a brief description of the working of the chief legislative organ as regards the making of laws, settling of cases, &c. Their methods of administering the law are as follows: Any private person, free or serf, brings his case to the headman of his village, the headman takes it to the resident induna of the native district in which the village may lie, the country being divided off into a large number of districts, like parishes in England, though much bigger in area; the resident induna carries the case to the Kotla induna who represents that native district in the Kotla and the representative induna takes the case to the Ngambela who hears the case at his own residence. Should the parties agree to the Ngambela's finding the case is settled, but should there be any dissatisfaction the matter is discussed before the assembled Kotla, each party speaking in turn with their respective witnesses.

The divisions enumerated earlier in this chapter have each and all of them certain duties and privileges. The "Sikalu" is a Privy Council and consists of a score or so of the highest indunas. They are divided again into two divisions which have their respective duties. The "Sikalu" of the night sits together with the Chief in a very humble sort of hut, a good distance from any chance of eavesdropping, and these indunas when so employed do not "kandelela" when speaking to the Chief. The Ngambela is one of the night Sikalu. The Sikalu discusses any new law to be made or any important matter which it is necessary to keep very secret, and these discussions are always held in whispers and at a good distance from any likely shelter for eavesdroppers.

Arrival of the Nalikwanda

Photo by J. C. Coxhead, Esq.

The Secretary for Native Affairs and the late Paramount Chief

Photo by J. C. Coxhead, Esq.

The Sikalu of the day is sometimes taken on one side in the Kotla by the Ngambela if any little unforeseen piece of news or information crops up in any discussion. Their conversation is also strictly private and is held entirely in whispers.

The "Saa" is a much larger division of the people, and has the privilege of going to the Chief after dusk and discussing current topics with him, the Sikalu members being also members of the Saa. Any member of the Saa can talk when he chooses and about what he chooses. Should two start simultaneously the holder of the most important position speaks first. The Lukaya and Ikatengo are not allowed free access to the Chief but are only called into the presence of the Chief when required by him.

There are, beside these legislative divisions, several other divisions of the people headed by various indunas. On the death of an important person another person, generally younger, is elected to the place of the deceased; thus indunas of the same name have been at the head of divisions since time immemorial. These divisions are enumerated in order of seniority. It was the duty of the induna in charge of each division to provided a certain number from the division under him for tribute work for the Chief, or for raiding parties or anything else that might necessitate a large number of people being assembled together.

The first division is the Kabeti under the Ngambela who deputes his authority to the induna Imandi. The second division is the Mutakela under the induna Mukulwakashiku, third the Ngundwe under Noyo, fourth the Ngulubela under Katema, fifth the Kawayo under Namunda, sixth the Mbanda under Muyumbana, seventh Njeminwa under Kalonga. The first six divisions are Barozi only, but the seventh division comprises all alien people subject to the Barozi as well as the Likombwa or Chief's body servants and the less important of his relatives by blood or marriage. All these divisions and arrangements of the people are of long standing before the Makololo invasion, and were necessitated by the fact that as there was no known method of writing amongst the Barozi, every induna of the respective divisions had to act as index of the people under his supervision.

CHAPTER IV.
Barozi Industries.

The Barozi industries are neither numerous nor complicated. A simple people living in a state of savagery would not have any very great or serious wants. Living on the Zambezi, and in a low flat swampy country which becomes inundated yearly, boats were a necessity of life. The trunk of a large tree cut down and then carefully hollowed out and pointed at bow and stern, such were their first boats and so they are to-day.

In the course of time they found that a long paddle worked by men standing up was more effective than a short paddle worked by anyone sitting down, as well as being much more useful for work in shallow water where the paddles being cut long are available as poles for pushing the boat along. Of all the various trees used for boat making "mukwa" (a tree resembling an ash) is alone unsinkable, all other kinds sink on being submerged. Paddles are made of young "mukwa" as it has more play and give in it than other woods. Paddling itself is quite a fine art, and to be a paddler in the Barozi sense of the word is to have a more than useful knowledge of the science. Steering is done by the stern paddler assisted by the bow paddler, but by no means all of those who are good paddlers are capable of paddling in the bow or stern.

The Barozi say that they learnt boat building from the Batotela, but this is possibly automatically suggested by the fact that suitable trees for boat building are found a long distance from Barozi itself, either amongst Batotela on the Lumbi, Bankoya on the Dongwe, and Alunda and Balubale on the upper Zambezi.

Pottery.—This industry, since the introduction of iron pots and metal dishes, is fast dying out. At an earlier date large numbers of clay pots of all sizes were made. Considering that no wheel nor any instrument beyond the bare hands were used, the pottery work is wonderfully good. The favourite forms of work were big circular pots with wide orifices which were universally used for cooking porridge and other foods, and large pots with thin necks and narrow mouths which were used for keeping water in. These pots are very porous and are most excellent for keeping water cold during the heat of the day. The more ambitious workers (the industry is incidentally worked by women) used to cut patterns and daub red ochre streaks on their pots, this is usually done after the first baking. Children universally model animals, though very crudely, in clay, but few of these models are burnt.

The Nalikwanda

Photo by J. C. Coxhead, Esq.

Government Messengers and a Post-runner at Nalolo

Ironwork.—It is not quite certain whence the Barozi acquired this industry. They must have had some knowledge of it during their migration from the Congo to their present habitat, though when they first left the Congo it is probable that their implements were made of copper. The blacksmith work of to-day is mainly in the hands of the Batotela, Bakwangwa, Bankoya and Bambunda, although traces of it are found in all tribes, aboriginal and otherwise, who are included in the Barozi people. In a few places iron is dug for and short shafts sunk, but the main supply of iron is gained from swamps and the beds of small streams. The ore, as recovered from these sources, goes through a rough smelting process, being placed under a large fire of wood in a circular fire-place from which small channels are made in which the molten iron is run off. These channels end in small circular depressions which collect the iron and it is then left to cool off. The iron is naturally very impure and is always very soft, but on the other hand it is very easily rubbed up to a good degree of sharpness and is really much more useful and adaptable to rough work than well-tempered European steel. The iron when cool is then taken in hand by the blacksmith, whose knowledge is generally passed on from father to son. He uses rough pincers, heavy and light hammers and an anvil all made from native iron. Bellows are constructed by taking a large piece of wood which is trimmed down into two large circular basins parallel to each other with a long pipe running down from between them, a small hole from each basin leading into the pipe. A closed pair of scissors gives, on a very small scale, a good idea of the woodwork of the bellows, the two finger holes being the circular depressions and the closed blades the pipe. Over each depression is tied a well dressed piece of hide which is tightly tied round the rim of the depression or cup. In the centre of each piece of hide a light stick, about twelve inches long is attached, and by jerking these sticks up and down quickly, quite a useful draught is made. At the mouth of the pipe a nozzle of clay is made to prevent the fire getting to the wood. Only charcoal is used by the blacksmiths and this is made, by preference, from any of the harder red woods with which the country abounds. Spear heads, axe and hoe heads, snuff spoons and nails are the chief articles made, and a good blacksmith will embellish his work with all kinds of punched ornamentation.

Basketwork.—This is a form of work which is very nearly universal throughout the Barozi country, although certain branches of it are confined to certain localities. Plain mats made of rows of reed-like grass kept very close to each other by several parallel lines of bark, knotted to each individual piece of grass, are made all over the country. The best makers are, however, the Banyengo and Bambunda. These mats are about five feet broad and eight to ten feet long. A smaller mat, possibly introduced by the Makololo, is made of flat reeds which are kept together by strings of bark. The bark in these mats does not show as the reeds are strung on the various lines of bark. These mats are about two feet six inches broad by five to seven feet long. Another mat is made like the large mat mentioned previously, but worked throughout with a chequer pattern of dark bark so as to form squares, diamonds, triangles and, in the more daring efforts, to form crocodiles, men, horses, cattle and elephant. The best workers of this last form of mat are the Bambunda. Another form of mat is made out of undressed papyrus strung on bark, so closely that they are, when placed at a fair angle, practically waterproof, and the Bakoma who are the chief makers of this form of mat, frequently build their houses of several mats slung over a horizontal pole.

Crossing Cattle over the Zambezi

The Mokwai's House and Fence at Nalolo

Circular and oval baskets of white stiff grass with patterns of black grass woven into the white are made by the Bambunda. These baskets have circular covers and are really very well and artistically made. The black grass used for patterns is of two varieties, one kind being the pith of a very slender root belonging to a small bush, while the other kind is simply the white grass as used in the main construction of the basket, soaked and partially decomposed in water before weaving. The Bankoya and the Alunda make a very closely woven grass basket which is waterproof and which is much used in districts where clay is scarce, to carry and even to cook water. Grass baskets are almost universally made throughout the Barozi to carry grain, meal, sweet potatoes and other foodstuffs.

Woodwork.—The Barozi are not very proficient at woodwork, the neatest and best workers being again the Bambunda, Bakwangwa and Bandundulu who make stools and wooden dishes in large quantities. These are generally made out of a soft wood and are then hardened on the surface by being scorched all over with a red-hot axe blade, a certain quantity of fat being rubbed in after the scorching. The Bambunda are very clever at carving little figures of wood representing men, women, animals and boats, the Bambalangwi, Balubale and Alunda carve long hair combs and sticks in a variety of interesting patterns. The average Murozi can carve himself a knobkerry, axe and hoe handle, or the shaft of a spear, but their work is very plain though very neat and wonderfully regular.

The Bandundulu are the chief makers of boat paddles, though the Bambunda and Bakwangwa cut them as well.

CHAPTER V.
Barozi Customs (Mikwa).

The customs from infancy to old age and death, of the nation will be given first, and a few peculiar customs of certain tribes will be described afterwards.

Birth.—A pregnant woman on feeling her confinement near, has a small grass hut built for her at the side of her husband's house. There she is confined, no male being present, though other married women come to assist. Young women are not allowed to be present. The umbilical cord (kakombo) is cut close to the child's navel (mukubu) and a piece of string is knotted tightly round the navel to prevent further bleeding. The child is washed with cold water. The mother's thighs are washed with hot water, grass having been boiled in it previously. The afterbirth is buried by women near by. Certain roots are procured from the forest and soaked in water, the child being washed with this mixture every day for two or three months. The mother remains in the temporary hut for two months, women going every day to help her wash herself and child. After two days the husband may go to see his child but may not sleep there. Certain of the tribes absorbed by the Barozi have a custom that compels a woman, after delivery of a child, to sleep with two other men before returning to her husband. The Barozi themselves do not have this custom. About four months after the birth, if the child lives, conjugal relations are resumed, but if the child dies shortly after birth the mother mourns for a day or so, and directly she has recovered from the effects of giving the child birth, returns to her husband. Twins are not killed, nor are they considered unlucky. A child born deformed is killed, generally by the mother choking it by forcing the breast well into its mouth.

Triplets are very rare and are considered bad. One is killed and two left alive, the reason being that the mother has only two breasts. Children are suckled for nearly eighteen months. If it becomes known that a woman, married or single, has procured abortion, she is taken by the other women of the village and the hair of her head is pulled out by the roots. Nothing is said however, if a woman takes medicine to prevent pregnancy. If a woman gives birth to a still-born child a grass hut is built outside the village and the woman has to live there, day and night, for a month, only women attend her and bring her food, no man will go near the place. When the month is finished, the women bring medicine to wash her with and she is then at liberty to return to the village, but must sleep once with some man other than her husband, before returning to her husband.

Capture of a young Crocodile

Photo by Mrs. Cambell

Arrival of Lewanika's Subsidy at Lialui:
Carried by British South Africa Company's Messengers

Photo by J. Walton, Esq.

It is considered most unlucky for a woman to become pregnant while still suckling a child, and native tradition holds that the first child will always die, as after the mother becomes pregnant the milk then belongs to the unborn child and the bigger child will not thrive on it. Children are always carried on their mothers' backs, supported by a skin, until about two years old, after which age, if the journey is any distance, the child is placed astride one shoulder of the father and so carried. A child is never beaten till about two years old and after that chastisement is very mild. At six or seven boys are chastised by father or mother, but girls of the same age are only chastised by their mothers.

Arrival at the Age of Puberty.—Boys have no initiation ceremony, and circumcision, though practised among one or two of the tribes absorbed by the Barozi, such as the Balunda and Bankoya, is not practised by the Barozi. Girls have a ceremony known as the "Mwalianjo." Directly a girl has her first periods of menstruation, she immediately goes and hides, if living out on the plains, in an adjacent clump of reeds or, if living near the forest, in the bush near the village. While thus hiding she is not supposed to see or speak to a man or boy, and if one actually approaches through inadvertence, she covers her head with a cloth or skin until he has passed by. Directly her absence from the village is noticed by her contemporaries, the married women go and look for her and stop with her in the bush, singing and dancing. At night after dark, she is brought back to her father's yard to sleep, but at daybreak she is always hidden again in the bush. This goes on for a month. The women while dancing and singing round the girl beat her with sticks, not severely enough to do damage but hard enough to arouse the tears and lamentations of the novitiate. The married women also show the girl how to receive and how to comport herself during the conjugal embraces of her husband, one woman taking the man's part for the performance. Much advice is given her how to preserve her husband's affections. At the end of the month the women take the girl to the nearest water and wash her. One of the elder women then goes and turns the bridegroom out of his house and the girl is then brought and placed in the hut in the blankets, the husband recalled and the newly married pair left. The company then dance and sing all night, drinking and eating largely the while. In the early morning the women take the bride and cut all her hair off, and she is in all senses of the word, a married woman. This "mwalianjo" ceremony was in itself fairly harmless, although possibly a trifle coarse and vulgar from a European point of view, but of later years single girls who had not even arrived at the age of puberty used to attend these ceremonies and join in the obscene jesting that went on, and the married women besides giving good advice, also counsel the bride-to-be never to refuse the overtures of one or more paramours, as well as giving her hints of how best to hide these intrigues from her husband. Very few girls reach the age of puberty without being already bespoken in marriage. Should the bridegroom elect have died just previously or at the time of his wife's "mwalianjo" ceremony, the girl remains with her father and indulges in fairly promiscuous intercourse with the men and youths of the village, until a suitor turns up and marries her. Virginity is unknown and certainly not demanded.

Marriage.—As has been shown in the previous paragraph, girls are all bespoken in marriage many years before arriving at a marriageable age, and have, theoretically, very little say in the matter at all; the arrangements being made between suitor and father or mother. The mother's rights over her daughter are not so powerful as the father's. A young man arriving at an age when he considers it good to get married, goes to the parents of the girl of his choice (generally before she has arrived at the age of puberty), and asks their consent to his marriage with their daughter. If the parents agree, the suitor gives the girl a necklace of white beads and a blanket. The matter is then left until the girl goes into hiding for her "mwalianjo." No permission or approval is required from the suitor's parents, but sometimes a father while his son is still fairly young, will arrange a marriage for him. After the "mwalianjo" is finished, the bridegroom will give presents to his father-in-law and mother-in-law. The presents are generally an ox, a hoe and a wooden dish. The father-in-law on his side gives a shirt and a loin cloth to his son-in-law. The mother-in-law then cooks beer in large quantities and the bridegroom, his friends and relatives, the bride and hers, all drink the beer. The bridegroom also has certain obligations, such as cutting a garden for his wife's parents and building or helping to build a new house for them. During the performance of these duties the newly married couple live in the wife's village, eating the food of the wife's parents, but after performing these duties, the couple return to the husband's village, returning to visit the wife's parents occasionally but having their permanent residence at the husband's village. In case of divorce, the wife returns to her father's village. No compensation is due from the girl's parents if she is divorced.

Tax-payers

Photo by J. Walton, Esq.

Royalty travelling by Boat

Photo by Mrs. Cambell

Death.—The Barozi bury all their dead with the exception of lepers. Their reason for not burying lepers is the idea that if a leper is buried in the earth the ground will become impregnated with leprosy and everyone will die of that disease. Men and women are buried alike. The eyes of the corpse are closed and the knees bent right up to the chest. The arms are bent at the elbow and the hands placed palm to palm level with the mouth. A blanket is then folded round the body. A rough stretcher is made of poles and the corpse carried on it to the grave. Each district or collection of villages has a common burial place. If possible a corpse is brought to its own burial ground. But this is only done when the person dies within a short distance of his or her home. Corpses are buried the same day as death takes place. Men always act as carriers, irrespective of the sex of the corpse. The corpse is lifted off the bier at the graveside and placed in the grave, on its side, head to the west. The Barozi dig a straight square hole and a mat is placed tent-wise over the corpse. The clothes of the deceased are put in the grave under the mat, as well as a few wooden dishes and pots, the latter being first broken. The mat over the corpse is put there with the idea that no earth shall actually be thrown on the body, although as the sides get filled up, the mat eventually gives way under the weight and the grave thus gets filled up. Some of the burial party stand in the grave at the side, the rest push the earth to the edge of the grave. Those standing in the grave take the loose earth and place it gently all round the edge of the mat covering the corpse, raising themselves on the earth thus placed as the grave gets filled up. After the mat has given way beneath the weight of the earth, the grave is filled up. A mound of earth is placed over the grave and a few more pots and wooden dishes are broken and placed on top. The burial party and mourners then return to the village. On the path outside the village a small fire is made and the whole party, men and women have to leap over the fire as a form of purification. They then assemble at the deceased person's house and mourn. The mourning lasts for three or four days, and consists of sitting round the deceased's house and wailing. Cattle are killed, the number being in proportion to the wealth of the deceased, and the meat is eaten during the mourning. After the mourning is finished the whole party wash in special medicines. If the deceased is a man his house is broken down, but if a woman her husband still lives in the house, but the house is plastered afresh before he re-occupies it. No difference is made in the burial of a pregnant woman. The Barozi themselves make no distinction in burying hunters, though the Alunda and Bankoya do. The only people who have separate and special burial grounds amongst the Barozi are those of the blood royal. The less important members have a common burial place, but the paramount Chief and sub-chiefs at Nalolo, Libonda and Sesheke have each a village already built and selected, in the middle of which they will eventually be buried. In former times, many of the reigning chiefs favourite indunas would voluntarily submit to having their arms tied behind their backs and being placed thus bound into a boat which had previously been bored through in several places. The boat was then towed into midstream and sunk. It is also probable that in former days a number of slaves were killed with the deceased chief, but a natural shyness of admitting these things makes them very difficult to prove, while the sanctity as well as fear of approaching burial places of any kind, prevent any sort of exhumation as proof.

Certain of the tribes included in the Barozi, have different customs as regards death and burial, but they are very slightly different and the difference is hardly worthy of comment. The Alunda used to bury on platforms erected in the bush, but now nearly all burials are conducted similarly to those of the Barozi.

The Bankoya, Alunda, Bambalangwe and Balubale bury chiefs and indunas in their huts and, after so doing, generally move their villages a little distance from the old site. Hunters are usually buried outside the village, a short path being cut from the main path to the grave. Poles are stuck round the grave with the skulls of various wild animals on them. These tribes tie a long string to the corpse and keep the end of the string above the top of the grave. The Bambunda place a reed in or close to the ear of the corpse when in the grave, the end protruding above the top of the grave. Witch doctors and others are supposed to learn important secrets from the spirit of the deceased by means of a reed or string communication. Another custom among the Bandundulu is that of "bringing back" those men who stand in the grave placing the earth in it. After the grave has been nearly filled, the oldest woman in the village takes her hoe and places it on the shoulder of one of the men and pulls him out of the grave. Each of the men so employed is treated similarly. The grave is then raised to the necessary height. As far as can be gathered, though it is admitted that there is very little native confirmation, the idea is this: The oldest woman being very old and near to death can therefore get no harm from the dead. So she is chosen to affront the dead by bringing back from the grave, those people who were employed in filling up the grave, and who having entered the grave were as dead or as the property of the dead. The use of the hoe is symbolical of the digging out. The Alunda after a burial do not leap a fire as the Barozi do, but stand at the nearest bifurcation of the path leading to the village, and the oldest woman of the village brings burning sticks and passes them round the burial party. Here again, the employment of an elderly woman near to death and thus immune to the danger of the dead, is noticeable.

Having thus roughly depicted the four chief divisions of the life of the average male or female Murozi, a few points of their daily life as governed by custom will be now described.

Mankoya women dancing

Photo by J. Walton, Esq.

"Well in swing"

Work.—A very hard and fast rule is maintained in the division of the day's work although, as is usual with many native races, the greater portion falls on the female. The axe and the hoe are very emblematic of the different kinds of work for each sex. The man does all wood cutting in preparing a new garden or in building a house, while the woman tills the garden with her hoe, cuts grass for thatching with her hoe and mixes mud for plastering the house with her hoe. So emblematic are these two implements that very light and ornate axes and hoes are made solely for carrying when visiting. The woman does all garnering of grain, though the man builds the frame of the grain bin. Brewing of beer and cooking of food is woman's work, though young and single men cook their own porridge or employ little boys to do it for them. All mud plastering is done by women though the framework of the house, the building of the reed fence, and the thatching of the house is the man's portion. Grass cutting is chiefly women's work, but men often assist at it, reed cutting for fence and hut building is done by both sexes. A woman will fetch loose fire-wood from the bush but will not cut fire-wood down with an axe. All carrying is done by women on their heads but men always carry their loads divided into half, half fastened to each end of a pole which is carried on the shoulder. Women do all the carrying of water required by a household. All cattle herding and milking of cattle is done by men only, but the Barozi cannot give any reason for the custom except that it has always been men's work. There is a belief that if women enter a cattle kraal, it will bring on an immediate and untimely menstrual discharge, the only women who go near a kraal are therefore very old women or very young children. The most notorious exceptions to the above customs are the Alunda. These people will often admit they are the slaves to their women folk. The average Lunda woman's daily work is fishing, which they do by wading along the sides of streams, pushing a large wicker basket in front of them. The Alunda men use the hoe as well as the axe, and tend their gardens, grind meal for porridge, plaster their huts and do all the work that is generally supposed by other tribes to be women's work only. In speaking of the Alunda, it must be remembered that the Alunda living in the Barozi country are only a small portion of the main tribe, the larger portion living in Southern and South-western Congoland. All other tribes under the sway of the Barozi follow the customs depicted above, in the division of labour between the sexes. It will be seen by reference to Chapter IV that women do not share in many of the industries of the country; with the exception of the mat and pot making all other industries are worked by men. This, however, is only fair and just, as it will be seen from the preceding paragraphs that the larger portion of the day's work certainly falls on the women.

Salutations.—A great deal of the ceremony of salutations is being killed by civilization. The ordinary forms of greeting differ according to the status of the parties meeting each other. In a country where time was and is very little object, two people of equal status on meeting put down their spears and anything they may be carrying and squat on their heels. Right hands are clasped but not shaken, and a second grip is given after the first one, by closing the hand on the thumb of the proffered hand. This grip is done by both parties simultaneously, and is by no means peculiar to the Barozi, as the Matebele, Basuto, Bechuana and Xosa people all do the same. The Barozi, after completing the grip, clap their hands (kandelela) three times and then converse on various topics. If the parties are related or well-known to one another the two grips are given and then both parties join hands, the right hand of one holding the left hand of the other, and *vice versa*, a kiss is given by each to the palm of his friend's left hand. If very close relatives meet, besides this they spray each other with spittle. When a person of humble status meets an induna or person of importance, he or she steps off the path and claps (kandelela) until the big person has gone by. The Chief has a special salute for himself, which is also given to any envoy coming direct from him. It consists of every man greeting him by standing up and shouting "Yo sho" at the same time throwing both arms to full extent above the head, this is done three times, then all kneel, clapping their hands three times and shouting "Shangwe" (my father), "Mangwe" (my master), "Mawe" (my mother), this performance is repeated a second time exactly similarly and a third time, when the only difference is that the third time "Yo sho" is said on their knees. When women greet the Chief, they remain seated on the ground and shout "Ya shé" clapping their hands at the same time. These are the actual greetings although when the Chief moves about from one locality to another, large ceremonial dances for men and women take place. The clapping of hands (ku kandelela) is differently performed by the two sexes. Men bring both palms smartly together, the right hand uppermost and at right angles to the other hand. The women close the fingers and arch each hand, making a cup formation of both hands which makes a hollow sound as they clap the concavities together.

Mambalangwe "Nuts"

Photo by Mrs. Cambell

A great deal of respect is still shown to elders of both sexes. For instance, several women may be hoeing a garden and during the heat of the day one of the younger ones will go and fetch water in a calabash, or dish, for drinking purposes. On her return should there be other women waiting to drink, the eldest has the first drink, and this is not affected by the ownership of the dish or any other reason, except in the case of an old slave woman and a younger free woman when the free woman drinks first unless the free woman is a girl who has not been through her initiation ceremony when the old slave woman drinks first. Age has seniority, then married before single, maturity before immaturity. On the other hand, at a meeting or assembly, the younger men speak first on the supposition that their council is rashest and of least value, the old grey heads and deep thinkers having the last say. A father commands more respect in many ways than a mother, but there are other reasons for that more than the imagined superiority of sex. Chief amongst them is, that in a country of easy and frequent divorce, the children when able to walk and look after themselves, immediately belong to the father and gradually forget their mothers. But the principle of "respect for age" still has a great effect on the young of either sex, throughout the country. A youthful induna of much importance will still be exceedingly polite to older indunas of much smaller position.

A gift is always received by both hands, and the modern European method of holding out one hand to receive anything whatsoever, is unknown. This custom certainly arises from the idea that as both hands are held up to receive a gift, there can be no possibility of a stab or blow being delivered, as would be quite possible if one hand only was used to receive whatever was passing between two parties.

Feeding.—No unmarried women will eat eggs, as the belief is that if they eat them they will be barren. Nor will unmarried women eat the flesh of the pelican, because, according to native tradition, the pelican cannot, owing to strength and size of wings and extreme buoyancy, be pulled under and eaten by crocodiles, and if they were to eat its flesh they would not be caught as wives by men. No women may eat the monitor lizard (hopani) though men eat it and it is considered a great delicacy. The reason for this is that monitors look very like snakes, of which women are more frightened than men.

Men, women and children always rinse their hands before eating. This is the more necessary since most foodstuffs are carried from the pot to their mouths by hand. It makes no difference if a man is eating by himself or with company. After the meal the hands are rinsed again and the mouth as well. Men seldom eat with their wives, as a man who does so is jeered at and considered greedy, on the principle that being stronger than his wife he will grab the largest and best portions. Women and children, male or female, eat together, and little boys will eat with little girls, but grown up men practically always eat either by themselves or with men friends. Meals are eaten twice a day regularly, but sometimes more often when food is plentiful. The staple diet is a stiff porridge made of ground flour of manioc (a species of cassava), mealies (maize), red and yellow millet or Kafir corn. A sauce is made of fish, meat, wild spinach or monkey nuts, and the lumps of porridge are dipped in this as detached from the dish. Maize porridge is eaten generally with milk, sweet or sour. Meat and fish are preferred high, but fresh meat and fish are eaten when plentiful. Milk is a very popular form of food, especially in the thick sour form. Many kinds of wild fruit are eaten, as is game when procurable. The Nambove and certain lower classes of the Barozi will eat crocodile, but the better class Barozi turn up their noses at it, as they do at the wild cats which, however, are gladly eaten by the Mambunda. Food is eaten in early morning and towards sundown.

The appearance of the new moon means a general holiday. The day after its appearance no one goes to work at the gardens. In former times the "Ngomalume" and "Liwale" dances were danced in the villages of Nalolo and Lialui (the residences of the two biggest Barozi Chiefs) only, by men and women respectively, but this custom is dying out.

The ploughing and hoeing of a new ant heap is also the occasion (on the day after the ant heap is ploughed) for a holiday. The belief being that if a holiday is not taken the seeds planted in the new garden will die. This custom does not apply to ant heaps that have ever been ploughed before.

Certain tribes under Barozi rule have a custom which refers to the fidelity of their wives, but the Barozi do not make use of this custom. Should a man suspect his wife of infidelity he takes a little ash from the fire and when his wife brings the newly cooked morning food he throws the ash over it and goes out to eat with one of his friends. If the woman happens to be virtuous or, whether virtuous or not, wishes to give the lie to her husband's suspicions, she shuts herself up in her hut and bewails her lot or sulks, whichever her temperament may lead her to do. If on the other hand, she is unrepentant and reckless, she throws the spoiled food away and goes off and eats with her women friends.

The Barozi themselves have no form of blood brotherhood. They have a custom called "making a friendship" (ku ikeza bulikani). One man calls another to his house and tells him he wishes to be friends with him. If the other party agrees, the first man gives the other a small present. On the return of the second man to his house a return present is sent. This makes the friendship binding. After that if the first man is in trouble or need, he runs to his friend and the friend supplies him if possible, with what he needs or assists him to the best of his ability. Anything a man lets his friend have is a gift, and there is no obligation of returning it or its value, the only obligation that remains is that of help in the event of his friend wanting it. The subordinate tribes have a proper form of blood brotherhood. It is practised amongst men only. The two who wish to make the brotherhood get two cups of beer. Small incisions are made on the chest and a drop or two of blood is squeezed from the incisions into the beer. Each man takes the other's cup and drinks it, they then swear never to hate each other, never to kill one another should they meet in battle, and never to be angry with one another. It is believed that a man who kills his blood brother will die of leprosy.

Mat-makers, with Mats for Sale

Photo by J. Walton, Esq.

A Mambalangwe Family

Photo by Mrs. Cambell

There is a marriage custom that exists among certain of the subordinate tribes in Baroziland. When a woman is pregnant a man, generally an acquaintance of hers or of her husband, will go up to her and place his hand on her stomach, at the same time addressing his remarks to the unborn child: "You within, if you are a woman, shall be my wife, but if you are a man, you shall be my friend." When the woman is delivered this prophecy is carried out. There is, however, no record of what would happen if there were twins. This custom is probably learnt from the Batoka, but the Barozi do not practise it.

Another custom, also existing among certain of the subordinate tribes, is the obligation of a man to give a younger sister or cousin to his son-in-law, should the son-in-law's wife die or be childless. But if it is only a case of sterility the elder woman returns home to her father, as the marriage of two sisters to one man at the same time is not tolerated.

CHAPTER VI.
Barozi Riddles and Conundrums.

Conundrums are universal throughout the Barozi, and a few are given as examples. Most of them are lacking in humour from an European point of view, but the ability to guess them is looked on as quite an asset, especially among women and children. Each riddle is prefixed by the words "A-ko," "Here it is," used by the person asking the riddle. The person taking up the challenge replies "Keyi," which means "Bring it." These words are pure Silui (Serozi) and are used for all riddles, although the riddles themselves may be in Sikololo, Mbunda or any other tongue or dialect in use in any part of Barozi. There are not any permanent riddles, as they are generally made up by the person asking them, but there are a few certainly which, from the length of time they have been known and their popularity, may be considered as permanent jokes.

(1) *Question.* "Ku tanta mbilingwa ku uka ni mbilingwa."

"It climbs up and falls back."

Answer. "Ki kokwani ha ipahama kwa kota."

"An insect climbing a tree (still slips)."

(2) *Q.* "Kateli ka shangwe no malimba."

"My father's calabash has spots."

A. "Ki ngwesi."

"A tiger-fish."

(3) *Q.* "Ka ka bonwe fo ka felela."

"Something one cannot see the end of."

A. "Ki ndila."

"It is a road."

(4) *Q.* "Mbumu na mbumu ka kuwana."

"Chief and chief do not visit each other."

A. "Ki musitu."

"It is the forest."

(5) *Q.* "Tutanela twili ba mundi."

"Two huts in a village."

A. "Mele no akatana."

"The breasts of a young girl."

(6) *Q.* "Ka nwela ka tumuka."

"Something that dives in and leaps out."

A. "Ki silabo."

"A paddle."

(7) *Q.* "A lila ba likamba la walanda."

"Something that crys on the river bank."

A. "Ki maoma."

"It is the war drum."

(8) *Q.* "Ha ka siwi."

"Something that cannot be left behind."

A. ""

"A shadow."

(9) *Q.* "Ka be ka luma, ka be lu felile."

"If this thing bit, we should die."

A. "Ki munyako."

"The doorway."

(10) *Q.* "Kato ka shangwi ku longa."

"My father's boat is full."

A. "Likundi."

"A pod of peas."

(11) *Q.* "Ka kasa fezwi bu meti."

"Something of which the blood is never finished."

A. "Ki pula."

"The rain."

(12) Q. "I samba ka shemwa ak'a endi ni balelo."

"Born a long time, and yet cannot walk."

A. "Sitondo."

"A tree."

(13) Q. "Anuke a ku fukile utu kobela no ku kena."

"Boys dressed in white clothes."

A. "Ki mundali."

"Mealies."

(14) Q. "Lila la tau ha li iniwi ki nzi."

"A fly cannot sit on the stomach of this lion."

A. "Ki mulilo."

"It is fire."

(15) Q. "Ka bata mazwalelo."

"It looks for a place to be born in."

A. "Ki tozi."

"Pumpkin stalks (before they bear fruit.)"

(16) Q. "Mutala no ku sumenena."

"A well fixed fence."

A. "Ki mayo."

"The teeth."

(17) Q. "Ndundu no makumba."

"A bundle of bark."

A. "Ki lezazi."

"The sun."

(18) *Q.* "Namani ya zwalwa ka nako ye, kwamoraho a mazazi e na le manaka amateleli."

"A calf born now, in a few days has long horns."

A. "Ki mbututu."

"A baby."

(19) *Q.* "Lutondo lwa ka yengwa Nyambi."

"Tree made by the god Nyambi."

A. "Ki kuma."

"The papyrus reed (with tuft on top.")

(20) *Q.* "Mulamu wa Nyambi na mbulwa makolwa."

"The stick of the god Nyambi has no branch."

A. "Ki noha."

"A snake."

(21) *Q.* "Mulume a lebe a mane kapata matunga a bile."

"A long man cannot reach this country."

A. "Ki lihulimu."

"The sky."

(22) *Q.* "Komo i potoloha silezi."

"A cow that walks round in the mud."

A. "Mukwenyani."

"A mother-in-law."

(23) *Q.* "A mutulo u ku nengela a mbowela u ku nengela."

"The people of the north dance and those of the south dance."

A. "Matali a kota."

"The leaves of trees."

(24) Q. "Ku tina ku mukelekete, mukelekete ku choka."

"You climb this tree, it breaks."

A. "Ki mutwa."

"The little thorn-bush."

(25) Q. "Ka ka muenwa mwanda."

"You cannot see any trace of it."

A. "Ki mundu."

"It is the watersnail."

(26) Q. "Ndo nambulwa mwelo."

"The house that has no door."

A. "Liki."

"An egg."

(27) Q. "Ka lubilo ku siya sitimela."

"What runs quicker than a train?"

A. "Ki pilu."

"The heart."

(28) Q. "Mwandu ya ngulubati ha ku keni lishingwa zepeli."

"No two logs can enter this old man's house."

A. "Lisuba la ndonga."

"The eye of a needle."

Gang of Natives proceeding to the Mines in Southern Rhodesia

Photo by Mrs. Cambell

CHAPTER VII.
Barozi Songs and Dances.

THE LIIMBA.

This is a purely Barozi song and is sung and danced by women only, to celebrate the arrival of a Chief.

"Sitengu nalili, masiku a nakene, ndendende."

Sitengu (a small bird that is heard before cock crow) has called, the night is finished. Yea! yea!

"Mukalelwa mweta sikawana moya, ndendende."

The one who is in trouble says he cannot free himself from his trouble. Yea! yea!

"Mufuma mweta sika sheba sinu, ndendende."

The rich man says, I am in need of nothing. Yea! yea!

"Muwabelwa mushekasheka, ndendende."

The man who is glad always laughs.

"Mu siala munyima tayiwa mangwi, a kena ta liya mu yenda munyima tayiwa a tata ta ndoo."

He who stops behind, my master, is white like a pelican, but he who goes along (with us) is bright like a leopard.

And many other verses.

THE LIWALE.

This is a purely Barozi dance and is danced when the new moon appears, by women only, with drums and silimba.

THE NGOMALUME.

This is purely Barozi and is danced by men at the arrival of the new moon.

THE LISHOMA.

Purely Barozi, danced by men only, on the arrival of a Chief. In both these dances a large war drum is placed before the Chief, and the men shuffle round it in time to the drum.

Shooting Rapids

Ngonya Falls at Sioma, Barotseland

THE BUNYANGA.

An Mbunda song sung by men and women, generally sung when a hunter has brought meat, but also after the hearing of some case between various people. A few verses are:

"Tangwa lia toko nji ka bangila mwebwangi, wa ili musambwa lia ndonga, konja lala tulo njilinga bati mwebwangi na na welelo, buno buta njilinga chilapo."

The sun is set, I follow my wife, she has crossed the river, I cannot sleep, what shall I do without my wife? Yes, I will make a paddle of my gun.

"Njamba wa funda bilindi bia Kalunga, u yu wa funda umu."

The elephant digs holes of God, who digs here?

"Kwenda buchechi, kwenda na mema, mu zabule wino ngandu mwali umo."

Go carefully, go in the water, come out carefully, the crocodile is there.

The verse used chiefly after the settlement of disputes:

"Nena bwala tu nwe, kumi lia matemo, milonga tu andeka."

Bring beer to drink (and) ten hoes (as a fine) we will talk over the disputes.

THE MANDENDI FROM THE MANKOYA.

A song and dance for men and women, with drums accompaniment, danced for sick people.

"Kwa Mulala na Sikobela kwa ili lukambo yai, ya, yai, ya, we yai, ya, kwa ili."

To Mulala and Sikobela they have gone to dance, yes, yes, yes, yes, yes, yes they have gone there.

And other lines of a similar nature.

THE LIALA FROM THE MAKWANGWA.

A song and dance for men and women, with drums, danced for sick people.

"Mwaka bani fa bang'ambote matondo."

The year I will die, the medicine will speak to me.

"Ke' manene Nalwamba katondo."

The (medicine of the) tree standing at Nalwamba.

"Ni liat'aba kaowa."

If I stand there the insect kaowa (will bite).

"Tu kaiowani, tu kaiowani, mene sisingi kuli yowano tamba ni kalemwa ngandu."

Let us go and wash, let us go and wash, I do not want to go and wash lest the crocodile catch me.

And other lines.

THE NAIMBWE FROM THE MANKOYA.

A dance danced by the doctor, with the audience singing and beating drums.

"Mu kuchaba nkuni tu ka moni ba lubanda."

Let us go to gather fire-wood and to see the people.

"Shimu bombola mema, meme ye mema a kalambwi."

The cold water, the cold water of the river.

"Baulima na Balushangi mawa fulili kalangu kaluwi."

Balima and Balushangi, please make bells for dancing.

And other lines.

Food for Sale

The End of the Day's Journey

THE SEPERU FROM THE MASHUKULUMBWE.

A dance for men and women without drums.

"Si nibizi ka kapiololo, litaba kamuso li ta anduluka."

Do not call me with a whistle, the matters will be discussed to-morrow.

"Ha ni jeli fande haisi, mwa muzuzu ni mwa makozwana."

I cannot eat outside the house, inside yes, but not outside.

And other lines.

Besides these combined songs and dances, there are numerous songs that are sung to the accompaniment of the "Silimba" or kangombio.

The "silimba" is an instrument made on the pattern of a Xylophone—the notes are pieces of wood cut down very carefully till they are as thin as possible without splitting, each piece being fastened to a frame over long calabashes of varying lengths, the longer the calabash the deeper the note resulting from it. Each calabash has a small hole near the base, carefully covered with spider-webs to give vibration to the notes. The notes are struck with sticks (one held in each hand) with a knob of native rubber at the end of each.

The "kangombio" is a small hand instrument consisting of one round calabash with an open top on which a thin piece of wood is placed. On the wood a row of thin tongues of metal of varying lengths, is placed. The tongues of metal are fastened to the wood at one end and then run over a small bridge fastened to the piece of wood, the playing ends being left unfastened. The performer holds the calabash with both hands and strikes the notes with the thumbs of each hand.

A few of the songs used are given below. Like all native songs, the same line is sung over and over again till the performer wishes to change.

SILUI (SIROZI).

"Mangwalala a iya ku ndia a na eni."

The crows that come to eat my (body) are disappointed.

SINKOYA.

"Kana ka shiwa Kenda na kulila ipula Kambundu wa ya ndilila liye."

Child of dead people go and cry and ask the Kambundu (for food) because I am poor.

SILUI (SIROZI).

"I'anuke, I'anuke, I'anuke a Libonda."

"Iimbu ku lia mangambwa, tingulu, ku lia amamu'na ngulu."

"Mbu ku mwan'a lilolo wa twelanga meyi matungu."

Children, children, children of Libonda.

The hippo eats the pumpkin leaves and the sweet potatoes, and he eats the leaves of the sweet potatoes.

The hippo is the child of the lilolo (any place where three or more people sit together), he dives into the great waters.

SILUI.

"Mangwe she mangwe ku wabelwa."

Greeting to our master, we are glad (to see) our master.

"Wato wa ngi no yongela Kayenyi."

My boat is lost at Kayenyi.

SINDUNDULU.

"Kanitwa no mengo na kakayi."

I am alone my brothers are dead.

SINKOYA.

"Liyunyi lia lila ba mawa, lia nchingisha winga wa ku yanda nka yami, ba yaya ba ya shilunga."

The birds have eaten my mother, they have made me live alone and be poor, all my relatives are dead.

"Numwaka likuwana lia lile ba mawa."

This year they will eat your mother (and you will be poor to).

"Kasongo ku li mwene Shindi na litunga liendi."

Kasongo has gone to the chief shindi, and to his country.

"Nkaka lwabila wa matunga."

You my master are lord of the countries.

SILUI

"Ka nuwe mbu wa Libonda wa mona ka tu tjimba-tjimba."

The hippo of Libonda jumps in. You see him swimming.

"Ka mona wato ba lipe wa fulanga meyi matungu."

He sees a boat near the bank, he shakes the water at the bottom.

SINKOYA.

"Lwabila tu lienga nobe twa bula ku bwala maliata, tu liye ku shima ku malovu nkaka tu lenga nobe."

Chief we will eat your food, if you cannot give us presents give us meal and beer, Chief, to eat.

SILUI.

"Silwale, Silwale wa manitondo kasa lilume lile lile."

Silwale, Silwale of Namitondo is not a very big man.

"Kalume ka masumango, Silwale, Silwale."

A short man, Silwale, Silwale.

MBUNDA.

"Ipulani Kawanda, Kawanda, wa ya bika binakwata ku buta bwa ma ndundu banjitwila kabunga."

Ask Kawanda, Kawanda is gone who holds my gun and grinds my meal for me.

"Chinyanga wa ya, mama, soka ko komwalile ba ndumba na chisumpa, ba li munjubo na ba ningula."

The hunter is gone, my mother, shut the door to keep out the lions and the leopards, so say the people in the huts.

"Chilambu change, tangwa lia kuta na tate mukuzomba chilambu change njiambata mikila."

The day I go hunting with my father I will carry my blanket and (wild beast) tails.

"Liyumbo," or Food-tribute

Travelling in Barotseland

CHAPTER VIII.
Barozi Legends.

There are many legends amongst the Barozi, very few of them are historical, and they are more like our fairy tales. Many of them have equivalents among other native races, though generally differing in title. A selection is given herewith.

MWALIYE.

A man once sent his relations through the country to find a wife for him. After many and long journeyings they found a very beautiful girl. Her mother consented to the marriage and she left for her husband's village, taking her younger sister for company. The girl had never ground meal since her birth, which in a country where all women grind the meal for the porridge, was a very strange thing. When she arrived at her mother-in-law's house, her mother-in-law told her to grind meal for food, as she refused to grind any more for her. Mwaliye replied that she did not know how to, but her mother-in-law insisted, so Mwaliye took grain in a basket, a dish and a grinding mortar from her and went to get water. When she came back to the mortar she said, "Alas, to-day I have become a slave!" She then began to grind the meal, and as she stamped it with the long wooden pestle, she sang. This is what she sang: "At home I do nothing but look at the sun, here I am turned into a big flour pestle." As she sang this, the foot of the mortar sank into the earth. She went on singing and her feet sank into the earth and the dishes sank in as well. Still she wept and went on singing. Then the mortar sank into the earth, and was finally followed by the pestle and the girl.

When her husband came back, his mother was very sad as she did not know what to tell him. A little bird came near the mother's house and sang a song: "Your Mwaliye has gone very far down under the earth with her basket, and her plates and her mortar and her pestle." When Mwaliye's little sister heard that, she ran to the place where Mwaliye had disappeared and started to sing a song: "Open up the hole! Open up the hole! My elder sister! Open up the hole! When she sings thus, she saw the sun! Open up the hole!" When she had sung this, they saw the top of the pestle appearing, so she repeated her song till at last Mwaliye returned with all her things. Then she told her husband how her mother-in-law had made her grind meal and he was very angry.

SABWIZA AND HIS YOUNGER BROTHER.

Sabwiza was supposed to be a very handsome man. He was also a hunter of great renown. One day he went hunting elephants with his younger brother. But his brother hated him and planned to kill him. They soon found elephants and began to stalk them. When they came close Sabwiza loaded his gun and got ready to shoot. Then his younger brother who was close behind him, caught him and killed him. When he was dead, the younger brother went home and told the people of the village that Sabwiza had died whilst hunting. The whole village wept for Sabwiza; as they sat wailing for him, they looked up at the sky and saw Sabwiza walking on the clouds carrying his hunting gear. Then he disappeared.

Shortly after this the people took the younger brother and made him headman in Sabwiza's place. He was given all Sabwiza's goods and Sabwiza's wife as well. But whenever he sat with his wife or eat food or did anything, Sabwiza always appeared. So the younger brother died of fright.

THE THUNDER AND THE ELEPHANT.

The elephant always said he was not afraid of thunder. One day the thunder told the elephant that he, the thunder, was the more powerful of the two. But the elephant denied this and said that he was the more powerful. Then the thunder said, "All right! go a long way off and bellow. If I hear you, then you are the more powerful." Off went the elephant for a very long distance, and trumpeted as hard as he could, but the thunder could not hear him at all. Then the thunder started. It made a fearful roar and the lightning flashed. Then the elephant was very frightened. The thunder called out to him and said, "Do not be afraid, it's only your blood brother." The thunder slapped him on the back, but the elephant was very frightened and called the thunder his master.

THE WOMAN AND THE HYENA.

One evening as it was getting dark, a woman sat cooking her husband's food. A hyena approached the hut, the woman did not see it was a hyena, but thought it was her husband. She was holding the child in her arms. When she wanted to stir the porridge, she handed the child, as she thought, to her husband. The hyena took the child. When the woman had finished cooking, she said, "Give me the child and let me nurse it." But the hyena then ran off with the child.

When the woman heard her child cry out, she looked round and saw it was a hyena. The hyena ran away and ate the child. The husband hearing his wife weeping, came running and asked what the matter was. The woman told him, and they both sat down and wept for their dead child.

SINGALAMBA.

Singalamba was a hunter. One day he went hunting in the forest with his son. He did not kill anything, so he killed his son. After drying his son's flesh in the sun, he tied it up in bundles and went home. On the road home he heard a bird singing this song: "Look at this man who has eaten his son, when I get to the village I will tell them the meat is human flesh—Singalamba has eaten his son." Singalamba threw sticks at the bird and killed it; he then lit a fire and burnt it up. Further along the road he heard another bird singing the same song. He threw sticks at it again, but this time he missed and the bird flew on to the village. When it got there it perched on the roof of Singalamba's hut and sang the same song. When his wife heard the song she asked Singalamba if the meat were the flesh of her son, but he said, "No, our son has gone with meat to his grandmother." Then the woman sent to ask her mother if the little boy had arrived with the meat. Her mother sent back word that the boy had never come at all. So the woman again accused her husband of killing his son, and at last he confessed. Then the people were very angry at being deceived, and his wife took all her things and left him and went away home, and never came back to him again. The man soon after died.

THE STORY OF THE GREEDY WOMAN.

There was once a woman who loved eating above everything else. When the other people in the village usually went off to till their gardens, she put a stone in her cheek and pretended to be very sick with toothache. When the people saw what they thought was a bad swelling, they wanted to cure her by cutting it, after the custom for relieving swellings, but she refused, saying she was afraid of the pain. So they went off to the gardens leaving her behind. Directly they were gone, she spat the stone out of her mouth and got some grain, ground it, cooked the meal and eat it. She then lay down and slept. When the people returned they asked her if the pain were better but she always said "No!" She did this for a long time, but one day she was seen cooking food by an old woman who had also been left at home on account of ill-health. When the people came home this old woman told them how they had been deceived. So they made a plan to catch her. The next day that they went off to the gardens, they only went a little way and then crept very quietly back to the village and hid. When they saw the woman who was supposed to be sick, get up and cook food, they all came out of their hiding places and laughed at her. Then she was very ashamed for the rest of her life.

KABWELI.

One day some girls were travelling to the chiefs village to work for him. When they left their home a little boy named Kabweli followed them. When they saw him, they tried to drive him away but he refused to leave them. Again, when they had gone about half-way, they tried to persuade him to go ahead, but he refused and came along behind them. So they went on. Everyone passing them said "Where are you girls going?" They replied "To the Lumbi to the village of our chief Nangandu-ku-ambwa" (lit. the one who is called the Crocodile man). When the passer-by met Kabweli a little behind the girls, he asked "Where are you going, Kabweli?" And Kabweli always answered "I am going with these girls to the chief. I throw away the cinders." The work of servants travelling with their masters, amongst other things was to throw away the ashes. And so they journeyed on and whenever the girls slept, Kabweli threw away the ashes. But when the got at last to the chief's village they found the chief was just dead and that a lot of people had gathered to mourn him.

When Kabweli arrived and heard the news, he went to where the chief's body was and looked at it. Then he said, "Do not bury him for a little." The people listened and obeyed him. Then Kabweli went into the forest to look for certain medicinal roots. When he found them, he boiled them and bathed the chief's body with the juice. Then Nangandu got up and was quite well again much to the surprise of all the mourners. Then he gave Kabweli many presents.

THE GREEDY MAN AND HIS CLEVER WIFE.

There was once a man who was very greedy. He used to go hunting and fishing and whenever he brought back meat, he used to get up in the night, while his wife was asleep and eat it all, but when his wife got up in the morning and asked where the meat had gone, he always said the dogs had eaten it all up. So she went to the "Mantis" and told him and the "Mantis" told her to go home and put white shells in her eyes when she went to sleep. So she did this and when her husband got up to eat the meat, he looked at his wife, and thought her eyes were open. So he lay still for a little and then had another look, but she still seemed to have her eyes open. He did this all night and got no sleep, he was afraid to get up and eat the meat as he thought his wife was looking. At dawn he fell asleep and shortly afterwards, his wife woke up, took the shells from her eyes and went out and found the meat quite safe. Then she woke her husband up, but he was very sleepy as he had had no sleep, and he said "Go away, I want to sleep." So she ate up all the meat.

THE WOMAN AND THE HARE.

Once a woman lived in a cave. The hare came and asked her to marry him. She agreed. The hare was very proud and took the lion to see the beautiful woman. When the woman saw him, she sang "What does the lion want here? I do not like the lion, I only love the hare." Then the hare was very proud indeed. Every day the hare brought one or another of the animals to see his future wife, but the woman always sung the same song. But at last the hare in his folly, took a man to see her, and she fell in love with the man and married him. Then the hare wept bitterly for many days.

The Author and the Mokwai of Nalolo

A Mrozi Boat and Crew

THE DOCTOR SNAKE AND THE LITTLE BOYS.

Once a big chief took sick. His indunas called many doctors, but all failed. At last they went and asked the "mantis." The mantis told them to go to a certain cave near a large rock, where they would find a doctor. So the big indunas sent some small indunas. When they got there they sang this song, "Come out, come out, Mutombo! And all the people may see you." Now this Mutombo was a big snake. Then Mutombo put his head out of the cave, and, when they saw his snake's head, they fled in terror. Returning home, the big indunas mocked them and went the next day themselves. But when they saw Mutombo they also ran away. Then the little boys said they would try. When the snake saw the little boys, he came out and went with them, riding on their shoulders. When they drew near the village, the people saw the snake, and all fled in fear, until the boys told them it was the doctor. Then Mutombo cured the chief, and all the little boys who fetched Mutombo were given villages and cattle, and the big indunas who had run away were made their servants.

MANGE.

Mange was a chieftainess who ruled the Bakwangwa. Her brother, who was also a chief, hated her. The Bakwangwa also hated her, as she was a very cruel woman. At last she fell sick and died. She was buried by her people at Ituku, near a big swamp. Soon afterwards she came out of her grave in the shape of a very strong wind that broke all the branches of the trees. When she got as far as the swamp at Ikwiji she went down into the bottom of the swamp with all her cattle and people, and built her village there. Soon after this every one who passed by the swamp heard things that astonished and frightened them. Some heard cattle bellowing, some drums being beaten, people talking, women grinding meal, and many other noises. It is said nowadays if any one sees those cattle they die.

THE HARE AND THE ANIMALS.

Once upon a time there was a great drought in the country. So the animals all agreed to dig a deep well. This they did, and then went off to graze in the forest. A hare came along and filled his two gourds with water, and then dropped dung into the well. When the animals came back and saw the dung in the well, they were very angry, and kept asking one another who had done this dirty trick. The next day they went off to graze, but left the hippopotamus on guard. Along came the hare, carrying his gourds for water, and a small gourd of honey. He sat down and greeted the hippopotamus, who asked him what he had in his little calabash. The hare told him, and the hippo asked if it was good to eat. The hare dipped a feather in the honey and gave it to the hippo to lick. The hippopotamus was delighted, and asked for more. The hare agreed to give him more, on the condition that the hippo let himself be tied up fast to a tree. The hippopotamus was so greedy that he readily consented. After he was tied up fast, the hare drew water and threw some more dung into the well. When the animals came back, they laughed at the hippo for being deceived by the hare. Then all the animals took turn to guard the well, but the hare deceived them all and dirtied the well every time after he had drawn his water. At last the tortoise was left in charge. He lay in the water close to the edge and pretended to sleep. When the hare saw the tortoise was on guard, he laughed, and said, "I shall have no trouble in deceiving that old fool." So thinking the tortoise slept, he started to fill one gourd. The tortoise seized it. Then the hare beat him with his disengaged hand—the other was gripping the gourd—but the tortoise seized him by the hand, the hare tried to kick him, but the tortoise seized his foot, then he tried to bite him, but the tortoise caught him by the teeth—in fact, the hare tried everything but the tortoise held on until the animals came and found them and killed the hare for his impudence.

The Author and Lewanika

NYAMBI AND KAMUNU.

A long while ago Nyambi and his wife Nasileli were the only people on earth. Nyambi was a very clever person and made trees, rivers, animals, birds, fishes, and when he had finished these he made a man Kamunu and his wife. He found this man Kamunu was quite different to the other things he made; if Kamunu saw Nyambi making a spoon or working iron, he immediately did the same. So Nyambi began to be rather frightened. One day Kamunu made a sharp piece of iron, and threw it at a lichwe antelope, killed it and eat it. When he found it was easy, he killed many animals like this. Then Nyambi was very angry with him, and asked him why he ate his brothers in this way. Then Nyambi drove Kamunu far away. Kamunu stopped away for some time, but at last he thought Nyambi would forgive him, so he came back. Then Sasisho (a small unknown animal), who was messenger to Nyambi, reported that he had seen Kamunu carrying an anvil and a pot of medicine. Then Kamunu asked Nyambi to give him a place to plant his gardens. This Nyambi did for him. When Kamunu's mealies grew, the eland came and ate them, so Kamunu killed one of the eland. When he told Nyambi, Nyambi forgave him. Then Kamunu's dog died, and shortly after his pot broke, and again soon after this his son died, and on each occasion Kamunu came to Nyambi to get medicine to prevent these accidents. But Nyambi was afraid of making Kamunu too powerful, so he told him he did not know of any medicine. At last Nyambi got tired of Kamunu, and jumped over a big river to an island in the middle, but Kamunu cut down a big bundle of reeds and floated across on this. Then Nyambi called all the animals and told them that Kamunu was the strongest and cleverest, and would kill all if they gave him the chance. So the weaker animals and birds all agreed to run away whenever they saw him, and the strong animals said they would try to hurt him if they saw him. Then Nyambi told the animals to bring fire-wood and make a huge fire. When this was done, he put the Nyungu-luila-matanda (a large pot of special medicine) on the fire to heat. When the fire was very fierce and the pot very hot, he called all the animals and Kamunu to see who could take the pot off the fire. The animals all tried in vain. Then Kamunu saw how hot it was, and threw water on the fire, and, taking a bundle of grass well soaked in water, he lifted the pot up with the grass and took it off the fire. Thus Nyambi showed the animals how wise Kamunu was. Soon Nyambi got so frightened of the cleverness of man that he called the spider to spin a thread from the earth to the sky, and by this means Nyambi went to live in the skies. Nyambi is the god of the Barozi, while Kamunu is the first man on earth.

THE HARE AND THE CROCODILE.

The hare used to live on an island with the tiger-cats. He used to look after their camp and all the fish they caught. One day the hare stole the fish and ate them. He then tied himself up with ropes of twisted grass, and began to bawl at the top of his voice "Mawe! (my mother) Shangwe (my father) come and untie me." When the tiger-cats came back, they found him thus, and asked him who had done it, and who had stolen the fish. The hare told them it was some strange people whom he did not know. So the next day one of the tiger-cats hid instead of going with the others, and saw the hare steal the fish and tie himself up. When the others heard this they got up in the middle of the night and left the island. When the hare woke, he found them gone, and no boat left for him to cross in. At the river bank he saw a crocodile, so he said, "Old cripple, carry me over to the other side!" So the crocodile agreed. As they were going over, the hare said, "Phew! Crocodile, you stink." The crocodile said, "What is that you say?" The hare said, "I only said you make a splendid boat and swim very well." When they got to the bank the hare jumped on to the shore and told the crocodile to put mud on his back and lie at the edge of the water. Then the hare went off and found the hyena. He told the hyena that he knew of a splendid bit of meat which he would share with him if only he would take it to the water and wash it. The hare then took the hyena and showed him the crocodile's head by the water, and said, "There it is." The hyena could not see the rest of the crocodile's body because of the mud on it. So he went and made a grab at the meat. Then the hare called out to the crocodile: "There's the meat I promised you;" so the crocodile seized the hyena and ate him.

A Mumbunda Witch Doctor telling Fortunes

A Barotse Village

Photo by J. Walton, Esq.

CHAPTER IX.
Barozi Laws.

The ancient laws and customs of the Barozi are respected by the Administration as long as there is nothing repugnant in them to the ideas of justice as represented by the present standards of British Law. It is endeavoured in this chapter to give a brief outline of the more important of their laws with the penalties ensuing on a breach thereof, as in vogue before the arrival of the present Administration.

Homicide was not punishable by any fixed penalty, and no difference was made between murder and manslaughter. The penalty lay in the hands of relatives of the deceased, who could do one of four things to the guilty party, viz., to kill the guilty, to fine him, to take him as a slave or to let the matter drop. The last mentioned was naturally only done when politic to do so, the first penalty was generally resorted to when the guilty party was very poor and possibly useless as a slave. Compensation was nearly always settled by the assembled Kotla.

If a man was found slain near a village, but with no actual evidence as to the slayer, the village was held responsible for the killing and the Kotla placed a collective penalty on the village. A certain amount of danger lay in discovering a slain person at any distance from human habitations, as the finding often brought a charge of killing as its reward.

In a case where there was actually no proof, witch-doctors were called in, and some wretched person who had fallen foul of the witch-doctor or even of some of the relatives of the deceased, generally got fined, however innocent he might really be.

All cases of homicide are now adjudicated upon at proper Courts of Justice, duly approved of by the High Commissioner of South Africa.

Theft was punished frequently, more severely than homicide, but in a country where lock and bolts were unknown, this was probably inevitable. The guilty party had all his possessions seized by the aggrieved party and a clay pot was smashed, portions of it were made red hot with fire and the thief was seized and his fist tightly closed round one of the red hot pieces and firmly held there. This generally resulted in his being maimed for life, as the burnt hand festered and rotted away in most cases, while, even if it were looked after well enough to heal, the flesh and sinews of the hand were so burnt as to prevent the hand ever resuming its normal state and condition.

A kleptomaniac or an incorrigible thief was promptly helped into the next world. A first offence, if the value of the stolen property was very minute, was occasionally let off with a fine, but a second offence always brought the punishment of burning of the right hand. Theft cases are now tried by the Courts of Administration.

Adultery was punishable in various ways. The killing of the guilty couple if found "in flagrante delicto" brought no penalty on the husband. If the matter came to the ears of the injured husband later, the paramour was fined one head of cattle. There was no fine or compensation from the paramour if the guilty wife had gone uninvited to his hut, but the paramour was nearly always accused of having called the woman to his hut and could then be fined for the offence. The Barozi law has always been distinctly unjust on this point, but it was doubtless necessitated by the lack of morals among the Barozi. A woman could name any number of paramours to her husband on his return from a long journey or a hunting or fighting expedition, and these would one and all have to pay a fine to the husband, although the woman might have named them out of spite only. There is no such thing as rape amongst the Barozi. A man criminally assaulting a female child under the age of puberty, might possibly have to pay a fine to the girl's father, but carnal knowledge of an unmarried girl earned no penalty, and there is no known case of any woman or girl needing coercion, in fact the power to refuse, on the woman's part might practically be said to be non-existent, while the laxity or rather utter lack of morals certainly made the desire to refuse non-existent.

Start of a River Trip

Photo by E. S.

Interior of Lewanika's Dining-room

Photo by J. Walton, Esq.

Cases of adultery are still settled by the Kotla but, as there is always the possibility of an appeal from a decision to the nearest Native Commissioner's Court, the Kotla takes much more pains over settling these cases than in former times.

These three "Crimes" with their various sub-headings formed the chief cases settled in earlier days by the Kotla. Land disputes, which were rare, were nearly all settled by the Chief and as the country has ever been larger than the actual requirements of the people, disputes on land and water rights were practically unknown.

The Natamoyo's yard was always a city of refuge. Any law-breaker who could get away from the avenging parties, and could reach the shelter of the yard round the house or hut of the Natamoyo, was safe. "Natamoyo" in Silui or Sirozi means the "man of life," and thus his actual residence became a city of refuge to any wrongdoer. A day's sojourn at Natamoyo's yard was sufficient sanctuary and wiped away any obligation required by law.

Blood relatives of the Chief had practically, a different set of laws for their conduct. If one of the blood royal killed a man, he was fined very lightly as a presupposed provocation was allowed in his case.

If he committed adultery, he was fined the same as an ordinary man in amount, but as the royal progeny were the large stock holders of the country, the value of the fine was really quite out of proportion when compared with the same fine imposed on the owner of one or two head of stock.

If a thief was of royal origin, he was fined but never maimed like a commoner. The chief himself had no laws to submit to, but this freedom was largely counterbalanced by the knowledge that if his actions became too arbitrary or irregular, his life would promptly pay for them.

There is a curious custom which still holds good to-day, and which, though really belonging to the chapter describing customs, is introduced here as bearing on the laws pertaining to theft. This custom is "Kufunda" (Sikololo) or "Kushwanga" (Silui). This was the right of a man to his relatives' possessions. A man could take cattle, or goods of a relative, and the aggrieved party could not bring an action for theft against him. Should any one overdo the "Kufunda," the aggrieved party could warn his relative that he was tired of losing all his possessions and that the "Kufunda" must cease. After a public warning, any further case would be treated as a mild theft and a fine imposed on the guilty party, but this warning was seldom used, as a great deal of genuine generosity, or, it might be said, a genuine community of property existed amongst relatives. Nearly all other matters in the Barozi country are governed by custom. First, as a great deal of English law is based on some old custom, so do Barozi customs regulate decisions in any matters brought under the jurisdiction of the various Kotlas.

THE LAW OF SUCCESSION.

This law is particularly selected to be described here as a peculiar and solitary example of how the old Barozi law differs entirely from the similar laws of all the tribes now absorbed under the sovereignty of the Barozi. According to Barozi law, the heir is, if possible, a son; but failing a son, a brother. A father may nominate a favourite son as heir and he need not be the eldest son, but should he die intestate, the Kotla will generally choose the elder son as heir unless he is an outlaw or desperado, when a younger and better behaved man is elected. On the other hand the laws of all other tribes hold as the heir the sister's son. This, as is quite easy to understand, was caused by the looseness of morals of these smaller tribes, which meant that no man could be sure that the child born by his wife was begotten by him himself. It was argued that whoever was the father to the son of any man's sister, the son must at any rate have a certain amount of his mother's and hence of his maternal uncle's blood, and was therefore the most suitable person to appoint as heir. Comparing this with the Barozi law on the subject, it will be seen that although under Barozi law the nephew might be an heir if there were no sons of the deceased alive, yet the law or custom regulating succession in the other subordinate tribes, made the nephew heir in preference to all other possible heirs.

As a matter of fact, all estates (in which the ruling of the law of succession might affect other members of the deceased's family—to wit, the estates of wealthy indunas and headmen) come under the jurisdiction of the Kotla for settlement. The reason for this is that wealth is nearly always represented by cattle and as in ancient European times, the Crown was the only possessor of lands, so the chief is by repute the owner of all cattle in the country, and on the death of any person of importance who was in charge of a large herd of the chief's cattle, the Kotla had to step in to decide how many cattle should revert to the chief, how many were earned by the deceased as a reward for herding the rest, and how many should be left on the chief's behalf in the care of the heir. So, while the Kotla always hands over the bulk to one particular person, the other members of the family are also given a small share, while the estate often maintains the widow or widows—especially if pregnant—for some time, until remarriage or return to their parents releases the estate from such obligations.

A Mambalangwe Belle

Photo by Mrs. Cambell

CHAPTER X.
General.

Clothing.—The Barozi wear for the most part European clothing. The men wear what is known as "seziba" in Sisuto, or "sekupato" in Sirozi. This is made by taking two broad pieces of limbo and by joining them by a narrow piece. The broad piece is draped in front from well below the knees up to the belt over which it passes, the narrow piece turns down inside the belt, is passed between the legs and up the back to the belt under which it goes. Having passed the belt, the other broad piece is turned down from the belt to the back of the legs, hanging over the buttocks.

The women wear skirts made full at the feet and narrowing in to the waist. The wealth of a person is shown by the quantity of limbo worn in the "seziba" or skirt. The women like to wear anything up to eight or nine skirts, one on top of another as a large posterior is considered a great sign of beauty. Small children, after about the second year, wear a small dress over the genital organs, consisting of numerous strings of twisted bark. Further away from trading centres people are found in skins, the men with a skin in front and one behind, and the women with a kilt made of cowhide. Hides are used for blankets, but the European blanket is nearly universal throughout the country.

Personal Ornaments.—Few, if any of these, are of truly native origin. Brass rings are worn, if procurable, and ivory and bone ones. Ivory bracelets on the arms are, however, of native origin. In the old days, chiefs, members of the blood royal, sons-in-law of the Chief, and the wives of the Chief, were the only people who could wear ivory bracelets, but nowadays, anyone who can afford to buy, wears them. Ivory pins for scratching the head were also a royal privilege, but anyone who likes can carry one now. So in former days, the carrying of an eland-tail fly switch was a royal privilege, but this has also lapsed with time and the approach of civilization. Beards are worn by the men, but moustaches are seldom seen. No beard used to be allowed to be longer than the Chief Lewanika's. Even his son Litia, who had a longer beard than the Chief's, hid his beard inside his shirt when moving in public. Beads are universally worn.

Tattooing and Painting.—In former times red ochre was very popular as a decoration, especially for the hair but this is never used now. Tattooing is universal. The most common mark is the straight line running from the forehead to the end of the nose. This is done by men and women. The women also tattoo a black circle round each eye above the eyebrow and down to the cheek bone, this looks, when newly made, like the rim of an immense pair of spectacles. Women also cut rows of small gashes along the stomach about level with the navel. These were all supposed to add to beauty, possibly to draw attention to a clean skin. The women also cut a parallelogram of deep gashes above the buttocks right across the back, but this is done solely and simply to give their husbands a good grip on their wives when indulging in the pleasures of matrimony. Unfortunately, this place for a grip is not kept sacred to husbands only. A great deal of gashing is also done for medicinal purposes, which will be mentioned further on.

Religion and Superstitions.—The Barozi worship a god named Nyambi. He is, by repute, very cruel, and for this reason all children are given ugly names with the idea that if Nyambi should pass by and hear anyone calling "Katongwani" (the little hyena), "Kambotwe" (the little frog), "Namasiku" (thing of darkness or night), "Mubu" (mud) &c. &c., he would think a person with such a name as bound to be ugly and not worth killing. Nyambi is supposed to have a wife named Nasilele who is represented by the Evening Star. When the moon wanes, this is said to be from shame because Nasilele being jealous of Nyambi's attention to a younger wife, is trying to poison Nyambi. The new moon shows that Nasilele has been unsuccessful. Thunder and lightning, which is all classed as rain, is said to be sent from Nyambi. The lightning is supposed to be an enormous spur wing goose. Its wings beating against the earth cause the thunder and lightning, and the damage actually done by lightning is said to be caused by the spur of the goose's wing. A small table, about eighteen inches high, is erected in every village, and on this are generally placed a small dish of water and a few cobs of mealies or other foodstuffs. This is in case Nyambi should feel hungry or thirsty while passing through the village. The Barozi do not, however, realize a heaven. A dead man's spirit is either captured by a witch doctor as his servant, or else starts a career of its own—always of evil-doing. The spirits of the dead always work off any old scores that may be outstanding between the deceased and other people. Sickness, bad crops, accidents, bad luck, &c., are all attributed to the malignancy of spirits. To this day, cattle are sent as an offering to the grave of Mwanambinji, who in his day was a great chief, and who becoming scared of his brother, descended with people and cattle into the earth near Sinanga in the Barozi Valley.

A Mankoya Chief and Retinue

Photo by J. Walton, Esq.

Certain people are credited with power to make rain, to give immunity from lions, to cure all sicknesses and many other things, but they will, none of them, stand inspection or examination. All abnormal sights in the heavens, such as the appearance of Halley's Comet, which was very clearly visible in the Barozi country, are said to be signs of great trouble coming. The death of His Majesty, King Edward VII., was at once received as the misfortune predicted by the appearance of the comet.

Amongst the Barozi, monkeys are said to be human beings and the Barozi do not eat them, although some of the subordinate tribes do so. The "Lisikita" (grey owl) is looked on with great dread and only a few educated Barozi will shoot at it. Its presence is said to foretell the speedy death of some member of the village at which it is seen. The "Lisikita" is said to live on human bodies and is often considered to be a "Muloi" i.e., an evil spirit sent by some one to bewitch and kill an enemy. Great faith is put in witch-craft of all sorts. If two men quarrel, one will go to a witch-doctor and pay him an agreed price to bewitch his enemy. The natural vicissitudes of daily life all play into the hands of the witch doctor. A man cutting a bough, may get hurt by the bough falling on him, the axe may slip and cut him, a thorn in the bush may graze him and give him blood-poisoning, he may have a touch of fever, his cattle may die from bad grazing, all and everything is immediately claimed by the witch-doctor as a proof of the potency of his charm. The bewitchment is in some cases, effected by certain herbs being boiled in water and the man's name being whispered into the steam, in other cases, the doctor climbs a tall tree, faces the direction of the village of the party to be bewitched, and calls the party by name, in other cases some reputedly wondrous herb dropped near the fence or near the hut of the party will do the necessary mischief; in other cases, a wooden dish filled with human urine and excrement and placed inside the party's fence will effect the evil. Women believe that by rubbing dried hyena dung on a rival wife's blanket, the rival will become repulsive to the husband and will be driven away to the honour and glory of the other wife. A peculiar and very disgusting method exists but the origin of it is unknown and it is very rarely heard of. It may possibly come from the west from certain wild tribes in the Portuguese Territory. If a man wishes to strengthen himself to bewitch his foes, he cooks porridge. When cooked he takes it into his house and makes his wife strip and lie flat on her back. Each handful that he takes to eat, is rubbed on his wife's genital organs. Whether this is only done when the foes are relatives of his wife, or against any or all foes is unknown. The Barozi deny all knowledge of this, but a case of it has been heard of in recent years, and as it seems a little too peculiar to be attributed to the imagination of the wife, mention has been made of it.

There is a quaint ceremony attached to the yearly move of the chief from his village to his rainy season dwelling-place. It might almost belong to the chapter devoted to customs, but its similarity to the Old Testament story of the ark, has almost brought it under the heading of religion. It must be explained that the Barozi valley is a huge plain which is inundated during the wet season, from March to May, by the floods from the Zambesi. There is a legend that the first known Barozi chief "Mbōō" (Mwanasilundwe) had warning that there was going to be an abnormal flood. The name of this flood was "Meya-lungwangwa" (the waters are itching). So he built himself a tremendous boat of beams of wood which he laced together with bark and reeds. When completed, he got on to this with his wives, children, animals and servants, and went on until at last he reached the higher forest country where he was safe. The chief, every year at high water goes off to his village at the edge of the valley, in a very large boat, with about sixty people paddling in front of the boat and another sixty in the stern. The boat is called "Nalikwanda" and is always spoken of as a man, and when being prepared for the excursion has a "beard" made of plaited reeds hung on to bow and stem. Over the shelter ("lutanka") erected in the middle of the boat, is a big figure representing an elephant— the crest of the chief. (The Mokwai of Nalolo and Litia also perform this ceremony, and have a bull and an eland respectively as their crests.) The chief sits in the "lutanka" or shelter and eats there while on the voyage. Fire is carried on a small raised daïs made of clay, and the chief's war drums are carried on board and beaten strenuously throughout the trip. The paddlers in front, where they can be seen, are always relatives of the chief, those behind are the leading indunas headed by the Prime Minister. If a "relative" swaggers because he paddles under the eyes of the chief, there is always the retort that he paddles where he can be seen, but may not paddle at the back as he can't be trusted. In old days the induna in charge of the whole crew, had the power to throw out anyone who did not paddle well, and this is kept up to-day, though more as a memento of old times than for any inefficiency, one or two of the paddlers always being thrown overboard into the water, much to the delight of the rest of the crew. The whole trip is the most important ceremony of the year, and the "Nalikwanda" is accompanied by innumerable boats of all sizes filled with men, women and children. All present shriek and yell at the tops of their voices, and the drums are beaten as hard as possible. The resulting noise is better imagined than described. Every few moments a paddler of the Nalikwanda calls out "Ana moyōō" (People of life) and the whole crew roars "Wōō." This is done twice at a time amid the redoubled yells of the populace. Arrived at their destination, the chief lands amid the acclamations and greetings of his people. The same ceremony is employed for the return journey at the end of the rainy season.

A Traveller on the Zambezi

Photo by J. Walton, Esq.

Hauling Boats through Rapids

The Barozi have certain medicines to prevent pregnancy, and although they are not at all ready to submit these roots for analysis, they are by repute very effective. They have other roots to assist women to become pregnant, but these do not seem to be held in such confidence as the preventive roots.

It is certain that the Barozi, or, rather, the "doctors," have knowledge of many very effective poisons, but here again the lack of opportunity to hold post-mortems prevents any definite results being proved. One medical officer who held a post-mortem was ever afterwards charged with taking certain portions of the inside of the corpse away to make up into medicines for other patients, and it took several years to overcome and remove this belief. Amongst other poisons the Barozi prefer to use the dried brain of the crocodile, as this when properly dried and powdered looks so similar to the ordinary meal from which they make their daily porridge, that it is indiscernible when mixed with the meal, and the impossibility of holding a post-mortem directly after death prevents the efficacy of the poison being proved or disproved. The Barozi themselves swear that it is most fatal. There is naturally much reticence nowadays amongst them to disclose the poisons or their names, but there is one poison that is reputed to take two or three months to kill the person to whom it is administered. The person poisoned is said to feel no effects for two or three days, after which vomiting starts and lasts till death; at the same time the body slowly wastes away. This poison is administered in either food or drink, and is only known, perhaps fortunately, to very few. Another very favourite remedy for complaints is the firing of a gun—loaded with powder only—at the afflicted party. This is generally done when the sick person is unable to afford a "doctor's" fees. As guns are left for long periods loaded, it sometimes happens that the bullet is accidentally left in, and the patient is then freed from any further need of medical attention in this world.

Games and Recreation.—Recreation is taken by old and young alike. Adults and children dance on all and every occasion. A few of the dances, as will be seen, are for the different sexes, but the majority of dances are performed by men and women together; although the men generally group on one side and the women opposite them. Children have other games in which the adults do not join. The little girls make clay models like human beings, and use these as dolls; the little boys make models of cattle and play at herding cattle. The sexes join in many of their games. The favourite games when boys and girls play together is "Mandwani." The children go outside the village and make several little grass huts about two or three feet high. A chief is appointed, and indunas and other important people are elected, and a mock representation of the daily life at the capital is acted. Another game is "Chuku-chuku." A child picks up some small article and hides it in the hands, then holds out the hand, and another guesses what it is. A correct guess meets with much acclamation, wrong guesses being loudly derided. Boys are very fond of making small traps to catch small birds such as sparrows. Riddles (liyumbo, vide Chap. VI.) are very popular, but this form of amusement is not confined to children only, as adults are equally fond of asking each other riddles. Children play another game called "Mayumbo." A series of small holes are dug in the earth and some small object is chosen. This is taken up by one player, who also takes up loose sand and throws a little into each pit, the small object falling into one or the other of the holes with the sand. The game is to guess which hole the thing has fallen into. This game has a close relationship to similar games which are found from Suez to the Cape of Good Hope amongst all African tribes, and may tend to prove a common source of origin for all of them, although it is also reputed to be played amongst Arab tribes as well; and if this is so, it might suggest that the game was originally introduced by the Arab slave dealers who undoubtedly came as far south as the Zambezi, if not further. Wrestling is also very popular amongst boys, but no other fighting is practised.

Totems.—This is a subject that might well come under the heading of religion, as doubtless, in earlier times the family totem was held in great respect and reverence. To-day however, the totem is rapidly disappearing from the Barozi, and many young men will tell you that they are unaware of their family totems. This is very largely due to intermarriage and amalgamation with other tribes. It must be remembered that a child took the joint totem of its father and mother, when one considers this and remembers also that the father and mother in turn held the joint totems of their parents and so on *ad infinitum*, it will be quite easy to understand the extreme difficulty in arriving at accurate information from a naturally lazy and careless people who have, apparently, never had any methods of record. There is no doubt that the mother's totem predominates and always has done so, as cases are numerous of men marrying back to the same (or partially the same) totem as held by their father, but marrying back to the totem held by the mother is practically unknown. The totem laws were probably the origin of the fear and disgust of the Barozi to anything like consanguinity of married couples, and although to-day the totem is forgotten to a great extent, the marriage of relatives of close blood relationship is unknown, and the very idea of such a marriage most abhorrent. This is all the more striking amongst a people whose immorality is notorious and who might with justice be called unmoral rather than immoral. The totems, or such as can be remembered were numerous, all the large buck, the rapids of rivers, trees of the forest, fish, wild animals, roots and bushes and all the elements, were all held as totems for various families. It is worthy of comment that in the case of divorces where female children have been retained by the mother, these female children have assumed the mother's totem and dropped the father's totem. It is however nearly impossible to ascertain whether this is due to carelessness or is founded on some old law regulating the totems. To-day there is no certain knowledge among the Barozi whether edible totems such as buck, birds or fishes, were sacred to those whose totems they were, and thus uneatable or not, but an elephant-totem man will certainly not refuse a lump of elephant meat nowadays. The totem of the Chief's family is the "Namuchoko," a species of white pumpkin. This was the totem of the Chief's mother.

Architecture.—The round hut universally built by nearly all native races in South Africa, is most popular among the Barozi, although they say that they learnt it from the Batotela, an aboriginal tribe that were resident in the country when the Barozi entered it. The chiefs and big indunas built large square houses but this style they think was acquired from the Portuguese. The Alunda and Balubale who live to the north, and through whom the Barozi passed on their way south from the Congo, built square huts, but they also suggest that this was acquired from the Portuguese, so that it is a little difficult to determine what the true Barozi style of architecture ever was. Several of the wilder and more debased tribes build little grass shelters only, while the people of the Makoma country often build their residences of mats only. Some of the Barozi state that the true Barozi style of building was a long rectangular hut with a reed frame and walled with grass. The reeds were bent into a curved dome which was also covered with grass, probably a little thicker than the walls. This form of building is still used, but chiefly for travelling-camps erected en route for the Chief and royal family, and the dining-room of the Chief Lewanika is built on this pattern though very elaborately, and with mud instead of grass walls. Nearly all huts have a fence round them, the bigger the man, the bigger the fence. Grain bins are built of various designs; some are made on the pattern of a miniature round hut with a small roof which is taken on and off as food is required. Others are made of clay only and these latter stand four and five feet high. A large lump of clay is taken and hollowed out and as it dries, more is added to it till the bin is the required height. The grain is then inserted and a big cap of clay is put on the top as a cover. When the grain inside is wanted, a hole at the bottom is made and the grain taken out as wanted. The clay bins are only used for mealies, but the others for all kinds of food. All bins are built off the ground to escape white ants, mice and other vermin.

Portion of a Lubale Village

The Lunda Chief, Sinde, and Harem

Oaths, &c.—The Barozi are very prone to oaths. If a Murozi makes an ordinary every-day statement, he is disbelieved promptly and has to swear to its truth before he is believed. The favourite oath is "Ka niti—It is the very truth." "Fa" is another form which also means "It is the truth," but "fa" also means "there" and has probably got its value as an oath in a roundabout way by meaning "yes," there it is (the truth). The common expression of doubt is "Kauki." This is a common vulgar expression and means "(If you tell me a lie) may you be broken." Some of the missionaries hold that this word is very wrong, but it is dubious that it is any worse than the English "Go and be hanged," or any other vulgar form of disagreement. The Barozi have many of these forms of disbelief, "Lu kupazule" (you be torn), "lukung'a ne wena" (may you be injured), "Sijo so ta ja si ku pazule" (may the food you eat choke you) and many more. This form of oath-taking is called "Ku konka" or "ku kaule" and if carried too far is often a cause of squabbles and quarrels, but if real trouble is wanted in the shape of a fight, swearing ("Kulwaha") is resorted to. All swearing is done by invoking the private portions of the opponents' relatives, thus "Malete l'aho" (the testicles of your father), "Maboya maho" (the hair on your mother's thighs), and many other filthy suggestions, all enough to cause trouble. A man to swear at his wife or the wife at her husband is held to be quite sufficient grounds for divorce.

FOOTNOTES

[1] The father of Lobengula.

[2] With Sechuana prefixes, if Ba-rotse means the Rotse people, Bo-rotse = the Rotse country, Se-rotse the Rotse language, and Mo-rotse a Rotse man.

[3] See for a description of the Giant Sable and its habitat, and also an account of 'South African' elements in the Angolan Fauna, an article by Mr. Gilbert Blaine in the Part II *Proceedings of the Zoological Society* for June, 1922.

[4] As already mentioned, the '*Bo-*' prefix before the root -*rotse* means the country.

[5] I do not here agree with the author. The first Bechuana invaders or visitors about the year 1800 were from the Ba-hurutse tribe of the Bechuana stock. Their name became shortened into "Barotse."—H. H. J.

[6] The author spells this "Khotla." But in the original Sesuto word it is "Kotla."—H. H. J.

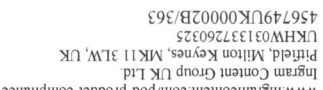

www.ingramcontent.com/pod-product-compliance
Ingram Content Group UK Ltd.
Pitfield, Milton Keynes, MK11 3LW, UK
UKHW031337260325
456749UK00002B/363